Christianity 101

A SIMPLER WAY FORWARD

By Reid A. Ashbaucher

Reid Ashbaucher Publications
Toledo, Ohio

REID ASHBAUCHER PUBLICATIONS
Toledo, Ohio U.S.A.
https://ra-publications.us

Christianity 101: A Simpler Way Forward
Copyright © 2020 by Reid A. Ashbaucher
All Rights Reserved.

No part of this publication may be reproduced, stored in a retrieval system, or transmitted in any form or by any means electronic, mechanical, photocopying, recording, or otherwise, without the prior written permission of the author.

The views expressed in this book are solely the authors. All resources noted in this book should not be seen as an endorsement of any kind towards the content of this book.

Due to the changeful nature of the Internet, any website address or link contained in this book may have been modified or deleted since publication and may no longer be functional as published.

All Scripture quotations are taken from the New American Standard Bible® (NASB), Copyright © 1960, 1962, 1963, 1968, 1971, 1972, 1973, 1975, 1977, 1995 by the Lockman Foundation, unless otherwise noted. Used by permission. www.Lockman.org

Scripture taken from the Holy Bible, NEW INTERNATIONAL VERSION®. Copyright © 1973, 1978, 1984 by Biblica, Inc. All rights reserved worldwide. Used by permission. NEW INTERNATIONAL VERSION® and NIV® are registered trademarks of Biblica, Inc. Use of either trademark for the offering of goods or services requires the prior written consent of Biblica US, Inc.

Scripture taken from the King James Version of the Bible.

Scripture quotations marked (TLB) are taken from The Living Bible copyright © 1971. Used by permission of Tyndale House Publishers, Inc., Carol Stream, Illinois 60188. All rights reserved.

Copyright 1992 Warren W. Wiersbe. "Wiersbe's Expository Outlines on the New Testament" published by David C. Cook. Publisher permission required to reproduce. All rights reserved.

Copyright 1989 Warren W. Wiersbe. **The Bible Exposition Commentary** published by David C. Cook. Publisher permission required to reproduce. All rights reserved.

Copyright permission can be obtained by the author through the following website: https://booksite.rcetc.com

Cover Image by 1195798 from pixabay.com

Library of Congress Control Number: 2020932591
ISBN: 978-1-7331399-4-6 (pbk)
ISBN: 978-1-7331399-5-3 (eBook)

Printed in the United States of America
U.S. Printing History
First Edition: February 2020

TABLE OF CONTENTS

Preface ix
Introduction xi

1.) The Beginning of Things 13
2.) The Gospel: From the Beginning.. 33
3.) Some Historical Teachings of the Christian Faith 55
4.) The Canon and Its Translation.. 89
5.) How the Local Church is Organized 107
6.) The Book of Romans:
An Essay Perspective on Its Teachings About the Church 133

Study Guide Suggestions 155
Acknowledgments 157
About the Author... 159

PREFACE

This book is a revision of the first and second edition of *The Christian Faith: A Quick Guide to Understanding Its Inter-Workings,* to include the change of its title and book cover. The revisions within this book are rewrites to parts of the book to bring clarity to its subjects and provide smoother reading within its sentence structure. Some paragraphs have been removed because of the nature of their content, bringing the book in line with less controversial topics, that should be handled in separate writings for a better understanding of the issues.

Having been a Christian for over 55 years, I can say, I have never been disappointed with God's working in my life. This is despite the ongoing spiritual warfare that rages between God and his already defeated enemy Satan, with God's people in the balance. The good news is that God's people have already won. The bad news is that there is always a cost within spiritual warfare. Jesus expressed it this way: "If anyone would come after me, he must deny himself and take up his cross daily and follow Me. For whoever wants to save his life will lose it, but whoever loses his life for me will save it. What good is it for a man to gain the whole world, and yet lose or forfeit his very self?" (Luke 9:23-25; NIV)

This book will provide solid information to those seeking a way forward in understanding the Christian faith or for those that want to know more about their faith along their spiritual journey. For those looking for material for their small group study, this would be a good choice.

The content contained in this book seeks to help individuals make better spiritual decisions about bettering their lives, by providing a clearer understanding of their Christian faith. But the facts on any subject are just that, facts. Sometimes facts can seem unimportant until they affect our interests, personal needs, or when God the Holy Spirit is working in our lives to bring about change. Therefore, I invite you to join me as we explore a simpler way forward and how that all works in everyday life.

INTRODUCTION

Those that come to God through Jesus Christ, come under all kinds of circumstances: rich, poor, single, married, widowed, divorced, young, old, orphaned, broken families, drug and alcohol addictions, abused, and the list could go on and on. So, where does one begin in this new life called Christianity? Many churches have educational programs, discipleship programs, counseling programs and they preach the Scriptures every Sunday. The issue is, for anyone to gain traction in any of these programs takes time. Building knowledge of any new subject can be challenging. There is a learning curve to any new subject and getting past that can take a while. New believers walking into a church listening to a Sunday sermon for the first time can be like picking up a good novel and starting their reading from the middle of the book, then trying to figure out who all the players are and what is the actual plot of the story.

If you find yourself in this circumstance, or if you are just someone that wants to know more about your faith, then *Christianity 101* is just for you. I design this book for those that know little to nothing about Christianity and need a starting point to gain some traction in getting up to speed on the topic. There are those that have been Christians for many years that do not know some things shared in this book. If you pick up this book and read it all the way through, you may find yourself way ahead of the game, and that is not a bad place to be.

So, what will we be talking about? This book will cover things like the nature of Christianity, its origins, its fundamental principles, its foundational teachings, the structure of the Church, and the Bible and how they came to be. This book may even answer questions you have had about Christianity for a while. Think of this book as your personal guidebook on the subject of Christianity.

The primary readers of this book will be those that are looking for ways to understand their faith, whether new to the subject or someone that has been at it for a while or someone looking at Christianity to see what it is all about. Either way, the result will be you end up with foundational knowledge on the subject and the next time you walk into a situation where Christian doctrine or teaching is part of the discussion; you will not feel out of the loop; you will not feel you just walked into the middle of that conversation but will be a little more confident in joining in the conversation. It is possible you might find yourself knowing a little more than the one standing next to you for the first time, perhaps to where you could help them along their spiritual journey.

The key to understanding this book's subject is to read it from beginning to end to include all the scripture passages referenced. The approach this book takes is to build knowledge in an organized manner and holds to the premise that there are no contradictions within the Scriptures, and therefore, for Biblical truth to be true, it must agree with all other Biblical truths.

As I stated in my first book *Made in the Image of God*, "summaries without study will lead to discussions without understanding;" so I will not try to summarize the total content of this book. As I have always believed if you don't ask the right questions, you won't get the right answers. With that said, come join me for Chapter 1; and let's see what we can learn from asking the right questions.

Chapter 1

THE BEGINNING OF THINGS

Sometimes life can feel like being in a maze, with the way forward seeming non-existent. When first entering the Christian faith, the learning curve can seem enormous. Within Christian discussions, it sometimes seems like you only can understand half the conversation, due to the lack of understanding terminology and spiritual concepts, not to mention trying to understand how all the subject matter within that conversation fits together.

The key to moving forward with learning any new subject is understanding the foundational concepts of the subject, then building on that foundation in an organized way—one piece at a time. Borrowing a concept from Jay Ashbaucher's book *Building a Life with God*, it's like building a house; you start with a plan, then the foundation, then you put in the plumbing, then the walls go up, we add windows and doors, then comes the roof. Once the main structure is up, you work on the inside details like insulation, drywall, counter work, then adding the finished work required to tie it all together.

This is the game plan for this book, we will start with factual information in a structured way, providing you information in an order that will help you see the whole picture that will make sense.

Our structure will begin with the Scriptures (or the Bible); which is not the foundation of the faith but is the instruction and guide book that tells us what the plan is and how everything relates and works together.

The Bible is a collection of sixty-six books written between 1446 B.C. and 96 A.D. by forty different authors over a period of about 1,500 years.

It was during the fourth and fifth centuries that the Christian church, in a canonization or selection process, compiled these books and were formally recognized for their authority as being divinely inspired as the Word of God within the Christian faith community.

These books were originally written in Hebrew, Aramaic, and Greek; and their canonization or selection arose in the understanding that God cannot lie—as declared to us in the books of Proverbs 12:22; Leviticus 19:11 and Titus 1:2.

St. Athanasius of Alexandria was a third-century Church Father, Christian theologian, and a chief defender of Trinitarianism—the teaching of the trinity. St. Athanasius of Alexandria wrote a series of doctrinal letters called *The Paschal Letters*. Within the 39th letter written in the year of 367 A.D., St. Athanasius raised the first question of which books should be canonized[1]—meaning which books should be selected to be part of the 66 books that currently make up the Protestant Bible that we have today.

This question was later taken up by a group of church bishops in the city of Carthage in North Africa. This meeting became known today as the "Third Council of Carthage" who met in 397 A.D. and decided on which books would be included in the current Bible, at the time they settled on 77 books—27 in the New Testament and 46 in the Old Testament. This included seven books known today as being part of the Apocrypha books that the Catholic and Eastern Christian Churches recognize as inspired today. Despite these facts, history points to the work of St. Jerome who was a Latin priest, theologian, historian, and is best known as the person who translated the Scriptures of his day into Latin in 382 A.D.

History has shown that Jerome's work was the true catalyst for finally determining which books would be recognized as divinely inspired. St. Jerome's work was completed as tasked by the Catholic Church; and it is known today as the Latin Vulgate, which was the first complete translation of the Old Testament from the Hebrew and *Septuagint* texts into Latin, and it included the New Testament books as they were translated from the Greek.

The *Septuagint*—represented by "LXX" (the Roman number for seventy) was produced by seventy Jewish scholars in Alexandria, Egypt; translating the Old Testament books from their original languages of Hebrew and Aramaic into Greek. This translation began in the third century B.C. and was completed in the second century B.C. It was seen as the Jewish canon or Scriptures of the Old Testament, and its use by the Apostles gave this work credibility within the first-century church.[2]

By the fourth century A.D., the canon of Scripture was closing, and divisions began to arise in the Christian church over what books would be included in what we now call the Bible—a Greek word meaning "The Books." When I say the canon was "closing," I simply mean which books should be accepted or rejected as divinely inspired, with no allowance for books to be added or deleted after final selection. So from the fourth century onward, different canons (book selections) began to be developed within both the Eastern and Western Churches.

It was not until the council of Trent—the 19th ecumenical council held by the Catholic Church in northern Italy between 1545 and 1563 A.D., as a countermove to the Protestant Reformation of 1517—that the Roman Catholic Church came to its final determination of which books would be included in its biblical canon, the Catholic Bible, consisting of 73 books. Within that same century, Martin Luther, a Catholic monk who turned theologian, made the final determination for the Protestant biblical canon, recognized today as the Protestant Scriptures—the Bible—consisting of 66 books.

Later, when we talk about translations, I will recommend some for your everyday reading and study purposes.

This book will focus on the Western Church canon of the Scriptures—recognized by St. Athanasius in the fourth century and finalized by Martin Luther, the Protestant reformer in the sixteenth century. You may ask if there is any difference between the Catholic and Protestant canons; and there is, just as there is between the canons of the Eastern and Western churches.

The biggest difference between the Roman Catholic and Protestant Bibles is found in the Old Testament. The Roman Catholic version includes seven of the fifteen books of the Apocrypha passed on by some early church fathers, like the books of Tobit, Judith, and First & Second Maccabees. The word Apocrypha means, "Hidden," and represents fifteen books written by unknown Jewish authors between 420 B.C. and 27 A.D; the period between the writings of the Old and New Testaments.

The "hidden" books were originally part of the *Septuagint*, with most of them being recognized as divinely inspired by the Roman Catholic and Eastern Churches. The Protestant and Baptist churches do not hold to this conclusion. Even though Martin Luther saw value in the Apocrypha, and printed them separately from his determination of the biblical canon, he did not see them as divinely inspired. Neither did Saint Athanasius of Alexandria in 367 A.D. Since these books were originally within the Septuagint, any decision to include them would not be unwarranted. However, they never claimed to be inspired; and the question of inspiration is not determined by origin alone, so we will further examine this issue in another chapter.

Having no personal background in the Eastern Orthodox, Syriac, Assyrian, Coptic or Ethiopian churches, nor the Roman Catholic Church, I will focus on the Christian faith from a Western Protestant Church perspective. This perspective comes from the result of the Protestant Reformation of 1517 A.D. when Martin Luther presented his ninety-five theses or doctrinal differences to the Roman Catholic Church. While others had pronounced some of these differences in earlier times, history credited Martin Luther for starting the Reformation. For those not familiar with the term "Reformation" it simply means, "the reforming of" or "to reform." It was the time in church history when Martin Luther, a German citizen who turned Catholic monk, had earned his doctorate and became a professor of Theology. It was at this stage of his life that Luther developed his reforming views within the Catholic Church of his day; thus, becoming the first of many reformers to follow. This was the beginning of what we today call Protestantism.

The Reformers argued that the church was then violating proper Scriptural interpretations of its teachings and daily practices. The reasons for these differences are not hard to understand, but the history behind the issues is not the purpose of this book. Instead, I will focus on the "Five Sola Statements" that united the Reformers and was the result of the teaching of Martin Luther. Listed below are the "Five Sola Statements" as supported by the reformers that proceeded after him.

1. Sola Scriptura—by Scripture alone.
2. Sola Fide—by faith alone.
3. Sola Gratia—by grace alone.
4. Solus Christus—by Christ alone.
5. Soli Deo Gloria—glory to God alone.

The importance of these statements cannot be overstated and should be understood as foundational teachings within the Christian faith. In short, the five statements are reflecting Christian teachings as summarized here: The Christian faith is lived by the authority of the Scriptures alone, not by any human authority. Salvation comes through faith alone, not through human effort or works. Our salvation is by grace alone, eliminating all efforts by humankind. Salvation is through Christ alone, eliminating all other paths to God. The entire salvation process is to the glory of God alone, removing all other credit that may be given to others.

PROTESTANT CHURCHES

From this historical understanding comes the organized Christian church that is represented by many denominations today.

Protestant churches represent a wide spectrum that is beyond this book's focus to define or even to list. However, to assist with any questions about the makeup of Protestantism, I have noted those church entities that are better known as representing their broader categories. Some names represent whole denominations, while others represent categories of churches; for there are many offshoots within Protestantism.

While Baptist churches reflect in many ways Protestant doctrines and practices, many Baptists would not see themselves as products of the Protestant Reformation. Instead, many Baptists believe their history came out of the first-century church and runs parallel to the rest of church history. There are full College courses and books on Baptist history, representing both sides of the issue, reflecting either being part of Roman Catholicism and Protestantism or being separate from that history. I have listed Baptists here because the "Reformed Baptists," along with a few other Baptist groups, recognize themselves as part of the Reformation.

This overall listing is in alphabetical order:

- Anabaptist
- Anglican
- Baptist
- Congregationalist
- Episcopal

- Evangelical
- Lutheran
- Methodist
- Non-Denominational
- Pentecostal
- Pietists and Holiness Churches
- Presbyterian
- Reformed
- Restoration

UNIFYING TEACHINGS OF THE CHRISTIAN CHURCH

The two unifying teachings of the Christian churches are the uniqueness of Jesus Christ and the belief in the Trinity of God. This simply means that all Christian churches teach Jesus Christ to be the Son of God, eternally equal in nature with God, who was born sinless, lived sinlessly and who died to pay the penalty of humanity's sins. He was then raised from the dead on the third day according to the Scriptures; he is now seated on the right hand of God the Father, and he will return to set up His eternal kingdom. All Christian churches also teach that God has revealed himself as existing in the form of three distinct persons: God the Father, God the Son, and God the Holy Spirit, all coexisting as a single divine being, essence, or entity.

At the international church council of Nicaea in 325 A.D., and later at the council of Constantinople in 381 A.D., these two unifying teachings were confirmed to be foundational to the Christian faith. It was from the council of Constantinople the final version of the Nicene/Constantinople Creed was written and universally accepted to be the central doctrinal teaching on these two claims, and it is still recognized in all organized Christian churches today, including within the Eastern and Western church views.

Here is an English version copy of this creed as agreed on in 381 A.D., [3] and used since 1549.

We believe (I believe) in one God, the Father Almighty, maker of heaven and earth, and of all things visible and invisible. And in one Lord Jesus Christ, the only begotten Son of God, and born of the Father before all ages. (God of God) light of light, true God of true God. Begotten not made, consubstantial to the Father, by whom all things were made. Who for us men and for our salvation came down from heaven. And was incarnate of the Holy Ghost and of the Virgin Mary and was made man; was crucified also for us under Pontius Pilate, suffered and was buried; and the third day rose again according to the Scriptures. And ascended into heaven, sits at the right hand of the Father, and shall come again with glory to judge the living and the dead, of whose Kingdom there shall be no end.

And (I believe) in the Holy Ghost, the Lord and Giver of life, who proceeds from the Father (and the Son), who together with the Father and the Son is to be adored and glorified, who spoke by the Prophets. And one holy, catholic, and apostolic Church. We confess (I confess) one baptism for the remission of sins. And we look for (I look for) the resurrection of the dead and the life of the world to come. Amen.

Modern Wording Version

We believe in one God, the Father, the Almighty, maker of heaven and earth, of all that is, seen and unseen.

THE BEGINNING OF THINGS

We believe in one Lord, Jesus Christ, the only son of God, eternally begotten of the Father, God from God, Light from Light, true God from true God, begotten, not made, of one being with the Father. Through him all things were made. For us and for our salvation he came down from heaven: by the power of the Holy Spirit he became incarnate from the Virgin Mary and was made man. For our sake he was crucified under Pontius Pilate; he suffered death and was buried. On the third day he rose again in accordance with the Scriptures; he ascended into heaven and is seated at the right hand of the Father. He will come again in glory to judge the living and the dead, and his kingdom will have no end.

We believe in the Holy Spirit, the Lord, the giver of life, who proceeds from the Father [and the Son]. With the Father and the Son he is worshipped and glorified. He has spoken through the Prophets. We believe in one holy catholic and apostolic Church. We acknowledge one baptism for the forgiveness of sins. We look for the resurrection of the dead, and the life of the world to come. AMEN.

Within the Nicaea Creed, please make a note of the statement: "And one holy, catholic and apostolic Church." This statement is in reference to the universal (catholic) church worldwide, and the word "apostolic" is in reference to the universal church founded on the Apostle's teachings as represented in the Holy Scriptures. This statement is not referring to the Roman Catholic Church or any denomination or local church.

IMPORTANT NOTE

It should also be noted that any church or individual that denies these two foundational principles, the belief in the trinity of God and the deity of Jesus Christ, as equal with God's nature, could not be classified as being Christian, even if they claim to be—verbally or in print. Why is this statement true? We will hold a discussion on this issue later in this chapter.

HISTORY OF CHRISTIANITY AND ITS SCRIPTURES

The Old Testament in the Bible is a collection of 39 books, which were written in Hebrew and Aramaic, the languages of the authors. The New Testament consists of 27 books, all written in Greek. Christianity's heritage has its beginnings within Hebrew culture and history, which start with the Old Testament. To understand Christianity, you must understand what the Old Testament reveals to us; for Christianity is a by-product of the covenant God made with Abraham—around 2,000 B.C.—through which Judaism and then Christianity was born. It is a long story, but I hope to make all this clearer as we move forward.

ORGANIZATION OF THE SCRIPTURES

Recognizing the Bible—a collection of books—as the basis for Christianity's teaching, guidance, and revelational information about God, we need to understand how these books are organized. This understanding should benefit those with an interest in further reading or research, and it should expel any confusion that may arise.

The terms, Old Testament and New Testament describe specific covenants (or agreements) between God and humans. I will cover the concept of covenants later in this chapter, but let us first see how the books are organized.

OLD TESTAMENT

The first five books of the Old Testament are Genesis, Exodus, Leviticus, Numbers, and Deuteronomy; known as The Pentateuch or books of the Law, which lay the foundation for the rest of the Scriptures. The next twelve books referred to as the Historical Books, cover the history of Israel until around 425 B.C. The next five books are Wisdom or Poetic Literature; though Hebrew poetry is quite unlike the poetry to which we are accustomed in western culture, for it is designed to teach and stress one point of view—God's. Seventeen prophetic books are next, with the first five being called the Major Prophets and the remaining twelve called Minor Prophets. These prophetic books focus on God's dealings with the nation of Israel and—to a lesser extent—the rest of the world, starting from their own contemporary era and reaching up to the end of our present world. They contain hundreds of prophetic statements concerning past events and events that are yet to take place.

The books of the Major Prophets are much larger than those of the Minor Prophets, many of which only contain just a few chapters. For example, the book of Isaiah has 66 chapters, while Jonah only has four. Lamentations is included with the Major Prophets despite having only five chapters; because it was written by the prophet Jeremiah, and it follows Jeremiah—his first book of 52 chapters. Lamentations is really an extension of Jeremiah's writings—mourning the destruction of the city of Jerusalem in 586 B.C.

New Testament

Within the New Testament, the first four books: Matthew, Mark, Luke, and John, are known as the Gospels, presenting the accumulative message of the whole Bible. These are followed by the book of Acts—a historical account of the development of the first-century church as it spread the Gospels' narrative and message. Next is the book of Romans—understood by many Christian theologians as a miniature Bible within the Bible—which covers Christianity's major doctrines (or teachings), while also explaining how these teachings' link with Old

Testament history. Romans is the first of thirteen first-century letters—sometimes referred to as the Pauline Letters or Epistles, which Paul wrote to churches or to individual Christians to guide and instruct them in the message God wanted to convey through him. The next eight books are letters from other Apostles and Godly men, who were chosen to convey God's message to the Christian Church. Many of these letters are warnings to the Church about false teachings originating from false teachers and from primitive pagan ideas filtering into the newly formed "body of Christ"—a scriptural term for the church. This concept of the "body of Christ" will be discussed in later chapters. Finally, there is the book of Revelation (or "The Revelation to John;" or "The Revelation of Jesus Christ")—as stated in the first sentence of the book. Revelation, written by the Apostle John, is the only book within the Scriptures with a catastrophic warning—declared in Chapter 22 verses 18 and 19—for those who would change, modify or delete any part of its original writing or intent. Please note the book's name is not "Revelations," for it is a single revelation or message from God to his church; not multiple revelations or separate messages.

Note that the book categories named within the Old Testament have been academically created for the purpose of better study methods, helping those studying Christianity understand the purpose and meaning behind these books—individually and collectively.

Jesus divided the Old Testament into three parts which he referenced as the Law, the Prophets, and Psalms, which is part of the remaining Scriptures called the "Writings." This is the Jewish view of how the Old Testament is organized. They see the Scriptural organization in the form of the Law, the Prophets, and the Writings.

Bible students throughout history attest to the Old and New Testaments expressing harmony with each other in their message and purpose—from Genesis to Revelation. This harmony in itself provides a remarkable proof to their validity, with forty different authors over 1,500 years without contradiction in their ultimate message. This is one of many reasons why the church holds these books to be divinely inspired, giving humanity an authoritative and purposeful message of hope and salvation down through history, all the way to the end of this age and beyond. We will discuss these claims in the following chapters.

WHO ARE APOSTLES?

Apostles were men chosen and discipled or trained by Jesus Christ to be his personal ambassadors to the world; and they were recognized by the first-century church for their authoritative, Godly leadership. Peter, John, Matthew, Mark—and later Paul—are the authors of most of the books of the New Testament.

The Apostles included the first twelve disciples whom Jesus chose to follow him, plus Saul of Tarsus, whom he personally confronted on the road to Damascus after his resurrection. Saul's name was later changed to Paul. Paul was believed to be later taught by Christ himself, during three years in seclusion, as reflected in Galatians 1:11-18—time which qualified Paul as an Apostle, and the same amount of time Christ spent teaching his original twelve disciples. Even though Matthias replaced Judas Iscariot, who had committed suicide at the end of Jesus' ministry (Acts 1:21-26), Paul could be seen as the true twelfth replacement Apostle, based on his selection and training by Christ himself, things that Matthias never was afforded due to the circumstances of the time.

God used Paul to write much of the New Testament, using Paul's background as a Jewish Roman citizen by birth; as a religious Pharisee; and for his extensive educational background in Old Testament teachings and law.

How Paul became an Apostle caused some to reject his authority, as he indicates in some of his writings. Nevertheless, the vast majority of the first-century church did recognize and accept his teachings and authority as God's Apostle, as does the church of today.

WHAT ARE COVENANTS IN THE BIBLE?

The Scriptures present us with two types of covenants—or promises or agreements—made between two parties. The first type is a conditional covenant which means that God attaches certain requirements to be kept as a condition for keeping his promise. The second type is an unconditional covenant which means that God places no requirements or any effort on the part of the other party as a condition of keeping his promise.

Covenants were sealed—or validated—by the shedding of blood. Old Testament examples include God's unconditional covenant with Noah: stating that he would not destroy the earth with a worldwide flood of water again. This was sealed with an animal sacrifice that Noah made as God instructed him; and God declared from that day forward, that the rainbow in the sky would be a reminder to all generations that he would keep his promise (Genesis 9:8-17). God's unconditional covenant with Abraham stated he would become a great nation; he would be given land for his descendants forever; and that all nations would be blessed through him. This was temporally sealed with an animal blood sacrifice, and it was made permanent through the death and blood sacrifice of Jesus Christ as expressed in Hebrews 9:16-27.

God's covenant with Moses is the Old Testament's foundational covenant that was considered conditional. Over a forty-day period, Moses wrote down the laws that God dictated to him, with the condition that if Israel would keep God's covenant—which became known as the Mosaic law—then God would make them a nation of priests and a holy nation before the world; and he would be their God (Exodus 19:5-6; 34:10-27).

The Old Testament records Israel's failure to fulfill the conditions of this covenant. It also records, in Jeremiah 31:31-34, God's promise of a new covenant with Israel that was unconditional: a covenant that

God would keep without any stipulations or demands on the Israelites or their leaders.

This new covenant was to replace the old covenant that God made with Moses and is the basis of the New Testament. This new covenant is validated by the death of Jesus Christ; and it is God's promise to forgive his people's sins; to remember these sins no more; and to place his laws within the hearts of his people. This is the Gospel message, the main message of the New Testament. It was later realized that the Gentiles (non-Jews) would be included in this covenant, which fulfilled the promise in Genesis 12:3, "that all nations would be blessed" (Romans 11:11-32; Galatians 3:8).

What was the main difference between these two covenants? The covenant with Moses was based on the promise made to Abraham and required regular animal sacrifices. But the Jews treated this covenant as a work-based system that focused on keeping the Law of God and forgot the element of faith; only to find that they could not keep God's Law through their own power; which furthered their guilt of sin (Romans 9:32; 11:6). The New Covenant, also based on Abraham's Covenant, is focused on faith in God's promised permanent forgiveness of sins. This forgiveness came through the crucifixion of Jesus Christ, the promised Messiah, who is our substitute to pay the debt of sin owed to God. We will speak more on this later.

Another very important covenant, known as the Davidic Covenant, is spoken of in Second Samuel 7:10-17. David was the second king of Israel, and this covenant was also unconditional. It states that David's throne would be established forever; and his kingdom would never end. How will this be accomplished? Jesus Christ, a descendant of David, through the virgin birth of Mary the wife of Joseph, will be its final ruling King, as the Scriptures state: "And behold, you will conceive in your womb, and bear a son, and you shall name Him Jesus. He will be great, and will be called the Son of the Most High; and the Lord God will give Him the throne of His father

David; and He will reign over the house of Jacob forever; and His kingdom will have no end." (Luke 1:31-33)

FALSE TEACHERS WITHIN THE CHRISTIAN COMMUNITY

During the eighteenth-century, new religious groups began to arise within the American Protestant movement, a trend that continues to this day. Though these groups call themselves Christian, they mimic the Christian church; and as you examine the Christian terminology they use in their teachings, you will find that they give these terms different meanings; changing them to say what was never intended by the original authors. Remember my comments about the unifying principles of the Christian faith? These groups deny these teachings, and would never agree to the Creed statements of 381 A.D. Yet they still deceive many people today.

Who are these groups? We refer to them as "Religious Cults" in the academic study of religion. If you take a course in "World Religions" through a Christian University, you will not find them listed as world religions. Why? Other world religions make no claim to be Christian, but these religious cults all make claims to some form of Christianity, or that they are the true way to God with no need of Jesus' sacrifice. Walter Martin, the author of the first edition of the *Kingdom of the Cults*, defines a religious cult as a group of people who follow one person's private interpretation of the Scriptures.

Some of these groups print their own version of the Bible or claim that their own doctrinal books or literature have equal standing and authority with the Scriptures, which allows them to claim their teaching as religious doctrinal truth. This is despite these teachings being contrary to the original Scripture's intent, and to the historical teachings of the Christian faith. This is not the same as disagreeing over how Scripture should be interpreted, which happens within the Christian church, and is why we have different denominations, which we will speak to later. Who are these groups? Here are the world's three most prominent:

- Mormons—who follow the teachings of Joseph Smith and Brigham Young.

- Jehovah Witnesses—who follow the teachings of Charles T. Russell and J. F. Rutherford.

- Christian Science—that follows the teachings of Mary Baker Eddy.

My purpose in listing these groups is not to be derogatory or condescending. My only intent in providing this list is to help you understand what is or is not considered historical Christianity as revealed through the Scriptures. This is why it is important to understand, biblically, what the term "Christian" really means. To this end, it will help to restate my explanation expressed in my first book.

According to Acts 11:26, the disciples of Jesus Christ were first called Christians in Antioch. In Acts 26:28, King Agrippa told the Apostle Paul that he had almost persuaded him to become a Christian. If you review the context of this word as used in these passages, you will find that it is directly tied to the person and work of Jesus Christ. Therefore, Christians are those who believe that Christ is God incarnate and God's only Son. If this is truly one's position, then one would have no issues with the Gospel message, as proclaimed by Christ himself, as represented in the four Gospel books of the Scriptures. According to the Scriptures, if one denies that Jesus Christ is God or believes Jesus Christ not to be equal in nature with God the Father, then by definition that person could not be classified as a Christian (1 John 2:18-23; 4:1-3; 5:20; 2 John v7-9).[4]

IN SUMMARY

What I have tried to express here is a brief historical outline of where the canon of Scripture came from and how we should understand the term "canon" as used in this chapter. As a review, we should understand the term "canon" to mean a select group of books recognized by the Christian church to be the authoritative and divinely inspired Word of God in their original form. This is important because, for any belief system to have any meaning, it must have some authoritative purpose and assurance behind it. For the Christian faith; that authoritative voice is the creator God, who has revealed himself through his creation, through the Holy Spirit and through His written word (the Scriptures) to humanity, who were made in God's image. It should also be noted that God the Holy Spirit does not contradict in our hearts what he has inspired to be written in the Scriptures—the Bible. Therefore, we are told to test the spirits to see who they represent—God or false prophets and teachers. (1 John 4:1-3)

I have not tried to give a full dissertation on canonization, or a complete historical perspective on the Eastern and the Western Church. My goal is to give a quick guide to the Christian faith, and hopefully to shed some light for new Christians; for anyone searching for faith; and for older Christians who have never been taught or discipled in the faith.

As we move forward, we will further discuss the Protestant canon and its translation into other languages, and make recommendations in selecting translations for your personal use.

This chapter has not addressed how to become a Christian; nor other major teachings of the faith; or how the faith should be practiced in everyday life. Instead, I have tried to summarize the foundational unifying teachings of Christianity, emphasizing if one does not recognize and accept these two foundational principles, one could never be part of the Christian faith. These principles are not just a matter of faith, they are also a matter of the truthfulness of God's words to us, as we read and understand the Scriptures. So, with all this said, come join me for Chapter 2. Let us look at the primary message of the Christian faith; test its meaning; and trace from its origins through to this present-day.

Chapter Endnotes

1. http://www.bible-researcher.com/athanasius.html (Link note added for additional information for the reader.)

2. http://www.septuagint.net/ (Link note added for additional information for the reader.)

3. Wilhelm, Joseph, *The Nicene Creed*, The Catholic Encyclopedia. Vol. 11. (New York: Robert Appleton Company, 1911.) [database on line]; available from http://www.newadvent.org/cathen/11049a.htm; Internet; accessed 4 July 2016.

4. Reid A. Ashbaucher, *Made in the Image of God: Understanding the Nature of God and Mankind in a Changing World*, 2d. rev. ed. (Toledo, Ohio: Reid Ashbaucher, 2017), 40.

Chapter 2

THE GOSPEL: FROM THE BEGINNING

The New Testament's first four books—Matthew, Mark, Luke, and John—are called the Gospels. This term simply means: "good news" or "good message," and describes how God the Father sent his only Son Jesus Christ into the world to be revealed as God in human flesh: to die as a sacrifice, to secure the forgiveness for our sins against God, and then to be resurrected—or raised from the dead after three days. Jesus' death and resurrection ultimately offers us in this life meaning and purpose and provides us eternal life with God to come.

This message was first proclaimed by John the Baptist, of whom Jesus said, "... among those born of women there has not arisen anyone greater ..." (Matthew 11:11) and secondly by Jesus himself. John the Baptist's message of the Gospel is recorded for us as follows:

> Now while the people were in a state of expectation and all were wondering in their hearts about John, as to whether he might be the Christ, John answered and said to them all, As for me, I baptize you with water; but One is coming who is mightier than I, and I am not fit to untie the thong of His sandals; He will baptize you with the Holy Spirit and fire. And His winnowing fork is in His hand to thoroughly clear His threshing floor, and to gather the wheat into His barn; but He will burn up the chaff with unquenchable fire. So with many other exhortations also he preached the gospel to the people. (Luke 3:15-18)

Mark 1:14-15 relates Jesus' message of the gospel in this way: "And after John had been taken into custody, Jesus came into Galilee, preaching the gospel of God, and saying, 'The time is fulfilled, and the kingdom of God is at hand; repent and believe in the gospel.'" The gospel message is the central theme of the Scriptures, with the four Gospels presenting four different unifying perspectives on Jesus' life, identity, origin, purpose, along with what the gospel message means for us.

The book of Matthew focuses on Jesus as the coming "King." The book of Mark emphasizes Jesus as the "Servant." Luke's Gospel presents Jesus as the prophesied "Son of Man." These books are referred to as the Synoptic Gospels, written for the same general audience (Jewish) and recording similar events over a similar time-line, providing an overall view of the historical Jesus. John's Gospel was the last gospel written, having a non-Jewish tone, as it reveals Jesus as the "Son of God" to the world.

As we think through this message, let us ask ourselves three important questions concerning the gospel: What is the purpose of the message? What is required to make this message work? Then how is this message validated?

WHY THE MESSAGE?

Genesis, the first book of the Old Testament, records how humanity was created by God: walked in fellowship with the creator (Genesis 1:26-28); managed all that was entrusted to them and lived within the boundaries established for them by God. Chapter 3 records how humankind chose to break God's boundary and go against his only rule for life: "don't eat the fruit of the tree of the knowledge of good and evil."

When we speak about violating God's boundaries, we are speaking about sin, which is any offense committed against God. Sin is also a breakdown in a previously good moral or ethical relationship with God or with someone else. When this happens on a human level, the problem may be solved simply by recognizing the offense and asking for forgiveness. However, in our relationship with God, there is a little more to it.

Within this relationship, we need to first understand that God can only function within the boundaries of his nature. This means that there are some things that God cannot do: God cannot lie (Titus 1:2); God cannot be tempted by evil (James 1:13), and God cannot deny himself (2 Timothy 2:13). God is also immutable, which means God cannot change his nature (Malachi 3:6). It is through the Scriptures that God's nature is defined for us, with the presentation of the following attributes:

- Omnipresent — God is everywhere at the same time.

- Omnipotent — God can do anything, with no one able to oppose him.

- Eternal — God is without beginning or end.

- Holy — God is separated from moral evil and is the standard of moral perfection.

- Love — God's holiness generates his care, compassion, forgiveness, mercy, and patience.

- Goodness — God is good by his own declared standards.

- Righteous — God is always in right standing to his holiness.

- Merciful — God has the capacity to be merciful towards whom he wishes.

- Wisdom — God is all-wise and understands everything: his creation, himself, and others.

So how do these facts about God's nature relate to people's sin? Remember what God said to the first human beings in Genesis 2:15-17: "Then the Lord God took the man and put him into the Garden of Eden to cultivate it and keep it. And the Lord God commanded the man, saying, from any tree of the garden you may eat freely; but from the tree of the knowledge of good and evil you shall not eat, for in the day that you eat from it you shall surely die." Because God's nature is holy, and he cannot lie or change his nature; his spoken words of death for man's disobedience must happen. If it does not, then God has lied in violation of his own nature, and he would then cease to be God!

Another important consideration is that God's words not only means physical death but also spiritual death. Spiritual (soul) death means to be separated from God in a fiery place called hell for eternity; which is described in Second Peter 2:4-11; Matthew 10:27; Revelation 20:11-15; and in many other scriptural passages.

Sin has permanently changed human nature: from holy perfection and the capacity to display God's attitudes, to pride and selfishness, which places humanity in a real crisis! (Mark 7:20-22; 2 John 2:16; Isaiah 2:17; Job 33:16-18) This is why the message of the Gospel is so important; for the good news is that God himself has provided the answer.

WHAT IS REQUIRED?

God declares that death is the required payment of sin: "For the wages of sin is death, but the free gift of God is eternal life in Christ

Jesus our Lord." (Romans 6:23) But, because God's nature is love as based on his holiness, God is willing to provide an answer. For the Scriptures proclaim, "Salvation is of the Lord" (Jonah 2:9; Psalm 3:8).

God's answer to salvation works like this. Because sin entered the world through one man called Adam, God would allow the penalty of death to be paid through one man called Jesus Christ (John 11:50-52; Romans 5:12-15). The catch is; the one paying the penalty for everyone else had to be as holy and morally perfect as God, who is the one requiring the penalty to be paid. And why did Jesus Christ meet this requirement? Because he shares the same nature with his Father—God, the creator—thus making Jesus God incarnate! This explains Jesus' statement in John 10:30: "My Father and I are one; " and his prayer to his heavenly Father in John 17:22: "We are one." The historical life, death, and bodily resurrection of Jesus Christ are known collectively as the Gospel—God's free and gracious gift. God's grace moves him to act mercifully toward us when we will never deserve such actions, as Ephesians 2:1-9 expresses here:

> And you were dead in your trespasses and sins, in which you formerly walked according to the course of this world, according to the prince of the power of the air, of the spirit that is now working in the sons of disobedience. Among them we too all formerly lived in the lusts of our flesh, indulging the desires of the flesh and of the mind, and were by nature children of wrath, even as the rest. But God, being rich in mercy, because of His great love with which He loved us, even when we were dead in our transgressions, made us alive together with Christ (by grace you have been saved), and raised us up with Him, and seated us with Him in the heavenly places, in Christ Jesus, in order that in the ages to come He might show the surpassing riches of His grace in kindness toward us in Christ Jesus. For by grace you have been saved

through faith; and that not of yourselves, it is the gift of God; not as a result of works, that no one should boast.

It is one thing to hear this good news, but until people respond, it is only half the story; for a gift can only benefit someone who accepts it. God says we must accept this gift by faith in Jesus Christ, with an attitude of repentance towards him. Jesus expressed this need for repentance in Luke 24:46-47: "Thus it is written, that the Christ should suffer and rise again from the dead the third day; and that repentance for forgiveness of sins should be proclaimed in His name to all the nations, beginning from Jerusalem." The Apostle Paul also declared, "... solemnly testifying to both Jews and Greeks of repentance toward God and faith in our Lord Jesus Christ." (Acts 20:21)

Hebrews Chapter 11—sometimes called the faith chapter—clarifies the meaning of faith and repentance. Its first verse says, "Now faith is the assurance of things hoped for, the conviction of things not seen," and it introduces examples of people exercising this definition of faith in their everyday lives. These examples are to help us understand this term as God intended; but to understand this information one needs to understand the history and circumstances of these examples, providing us a better insight into God's meaning of faith.

FAITH

"By faith Noah, being warned by God about things not yet seen, in reverence prepared an ark for the salvation of his household, by which he condemned the world, and became an heir of the righteousness which is according to faith." (Hebrews 11:7-8) Why is this a good example? Because despite the 2014 movie: "*Noah*"—an unbiblical fantasy and blasphemous in nature—Noah believed God's warning concerning a coming worldwide flood. In obedience, he spent an estimated 55 to 75 years[1] building an ark with his three sons in preparation for something he and the world had never seen—RAIN! Eventually, when Noah was aged 600, the rains came; and Noah and his family were saved (Genesis 2:5; 6:1-22). If you are wondering how vegetation grew if there was no rain, Genesis 2:5-6 records that a mist, which we would call morning dew, came up from the ground to meet the need.

"By faith Abraham, when he was tested, offered up Isaac; and he who had received the promises was offering up his only begotten son; it was he to whom it was said, 'In Isaac your descendants shall be called.' He considered that God is able to raise men even from the dead; from which he also received him back as a type." (Hebrews 11:17-19)

To understand the significance of Abraham's faith, let's backtrack to Genesis 12:1-3; 17:1-8, which records the everlasting, unconditional covenant God made with Abraham, promising he would make Abraham a great nation; provide him land that would be his forever; and that through this promise, all nations would be blessed. This covenant would be fulfilled through Sarah, his wife, and Isaac their only son. Several years later, God came to Abraham and commanded him to take Isaac to the top of a mountain and sacrifice him on an altar before God. Abraham obeyed God, but just as Abraham was about to plunge a knife into his son; God stopped him and provided a substitute sacrifice (Genesis 22:1-8). Abraham believed that even if God commanded him to kill his son, God would raise Isaac from the dead to keep his covenant.

Hebrews Chapter 11 interprets this passage as describing Abraham's faith as a type or a foreshadowing of how Jesus Christ, God's only Son, would be sacrificed on a cross for the forgiveness and remission of our sins. This is fulfilled in the story of the Gospel, with repentance and faith as a requirement to receive this forgiveness.

Galatians 3:8 match this interpretation as we read, "And the Scripture, foreseeing that God would justify the Gentiles by faith, preached the gospel beforehand to Abraham, saying, 'All the nations shall be blessed in you.' So then those who are of faith are blessed with Abraham, the believer." Here, the Apostle Paul is referring to Genesis 12:3, to confirm Christianity's ties to Old Testament history and roots.

Repentance

Repentance simply means to turn away from sinful thoughts or actions as defined by the Scriptures, and it is included within the Gospel preaching of John the Baptist and Jesus, which tells us the response God requires from us in relationship to his commandments.

Repentance involves three steps: recognition of a wrong committed; admission or confession to the one who has been wronged, requesting forgiveness; and taking action to avoid repeating the offense. As Acts 26:20 says: "... but kept declaring both to those of Damascus first, and also at Jerusalem and then throughout all the region of Judea, and even to the Gentiles, that they should repent and turn to God, performing deeds appropriate to repentance."

Summary of: "What is Required?"

Romans 5:12-21 (NIV) summarizes our discussion on this topic as presented here:

> Therefore, just as sin entered the world through one man, and death through sin, and in this way death came to all men, because all sinned—for before the law was given, sin was in the world. But sin is not taken into account when there is no law. Nevertheless, death reigned from the time of Adam to the time of Moses, even over those who did not sin by breaking a command, as did Adam, who was a pattern of the one to come. But the gift is not like the trespass. For if the many died by the trespass of the one man, how much more did God's grace and the gift that came by the grace of the one

man, Jesus Christ, overflow to the many! Again, the gift of God is not like the result of the one man's sin: The judgment followed one sin and brought condemnation, but the gift followed many trespasses and brought justification. For if, by the trespass of the one man, death reigned through that one man, how much more will those who receive God's abundant provision of grace and of the gift of righteousness reign in life through the one man, Jesus Christ. Consequently, just as the result of one trespass was condemnation for all men, so also the result of one act of righteousness was justification that brings life for all men. For just as through the disobedience of the one man the many were made sinners, so also through the obedience of the one man the many will be made righteous. The law was added so that the trespass might increase. But where sin increased, grace increased all the more, so that, just as sin reigned in death, so also grace might reign through righteousness to bring eternal life through Jesus Christ our Lord.

THE VALIDATION OF THE MESSAGE

To receive some new truth, or to learn that something good is going to happen to us, could seem exciting, but without validation, such messages are pretty much worthless. So let us examine three reasonable validation methods for the Gospel message. These methods are historical, prophetical, and testimonial. We should also remember the Scriptures also affirm how the Holy Spirit validates truth to every true believer in Christ (John 16:13-14; 1 Corinthians 2:10-14).

Historical

Genesis Chapters 9 to 11 describe the worldwide flood, with Noah and his three sons Shem, Ham, and Japheth surviving with their wives to re-inhabit the earth. For some years afterward, their descendants all stayed in the same region and spoke the same language. As time passed, they began to build a city, with a tower to reach high into the heavens, with the purpose of keeping everyone together as a people and to make a name for themselves. This was not God's plan, so he created confusion among them by changing their single language into many languages; which led to many groups of people scattered around the world with their own language.

We learn through the genealogies in Genesis that the Hebrew language came from Shem's descendants; one of whom was Abram, who was first called a Hebrew in Genesis 14:13.[2] The word Hebrew means, "To cross over." Scholars believe the Hebrew people were business nomads like Abram, and as such, crossed over the river Euphrates to settle as a people, hence their name.

Abram's family had left the land of Ur of Chaldeans—modern-day Southern Iraq—to settle in Haran, which is part of modern Turkey. In Genesis 12:1-3, God told Abram to go to the land of Canaan, which includes present-day Israel. It was from this land that God would make Abram and his descendants a great nation; a land that would be in their possession forever. Why would this be? Because it is this land that will eventually become the place where Jesus Christ will come to set up His earthly Kingdom (Revelation Chapters 20, 21). When Abram was aged ninety-nine, God changed his name to Abraham and established a Covenant with him; stating that many nations and kings would be among his descendants (Genesis 17). King David was one of these descendants, and Jesus came through King David's bloodline; facts that affirm Old Testament prophecies about Jesus' coming to earth as Prophet, Priest, King, Son of Man and Messiah—which we will look at in our next segment.

The next unconditional covenant was made with King David in Second Samuel 7:16: "And your house and your kingdom shall endure before Me forever; your throne shall be established forever." These are the words of the prophet Nathan, as God commanded him to speak. This Davidic Covenant echoes God's covenant with Abraham, and it will be fulfilled through the second coming to earth of Jesus Christ, who will establish his kingdom as the final ruling King. The fulfillment of all these unconditional Covenants (Revelation 20) is confirmed to us by the angel Gabriel as he proclaims, "Do not be afraid, Mary; for you have found favor with God. And behold, you will conceive in your womb, and bear a son, and you shall name Him Jesus. He will be great, and will be called the Son of the Most High; and the Lord God will give Him the throne of His father David; and He will reign over the house of Jacob forever; and His kingdom will have no end." (Luke 1:30-33)

The last of God's unconditional covenants was with the nation of Israel, in which he will establish his laws within them, and that he will forgive their sins and remember these sins no more (Jeremiah 31:31-34). This covenant is the historical basis of the entire New Testament; and it is best understood through addressing the question of how God puts his law in us; and how God permanently forgives us. These questions are answered through Jesus' death, burial, and bodily resurrection; and the indwelling of the Holy Spirit.

Jesus paid the blood-penalty for our sins and; by indwelling us; the Holy Spirit applies this payment to our lives, so we may personally receive his new nature within us. This new nature is a metaphysical part of us; a divine attribute that opens our understanding of God and his laws or protective boundaries, so we may become new creatures in Christ as described in Second Corinthians 5:17. This whole process is illustrated to us by Jesus' explanation of how the spirit world functions in John 3:1-15 and the Apostle Peter's comments in Second Peter 1:4. You can find a more in-depth discussion on these concepts through my first book, *Made in the Image of God*.

The covenants are thus fulfilled through the teamwork of the whole Trinity; otherwise, the Gospel is dead and ineffective—as the Apostle Paul explains in First Corinthians 15:12-17:

> Now if Christ is preached, that He has been raised from the dead, how do some among you say that there is no resurrection of the dead? But if there is no resurrection of the dead, not even Christ has been raised; and if Christ has not been raised, then our preaching is vain, your faith also is vain. Moreover we are even found to be false witnesses of God, because we witnessed against God that He raised Christ, whom He did not raise, if in fact the dead are not raised. For if the dead are not raised, not even Christ has been raised; and if Christ has not been raised, your faith is worthless; you are still in your sins.

Paul continues this thought in Galatians 3:1-9:

> You foolish Galatians. Who has bewitched you, before whose eyes Jesus Christ was publicly portrayed as crucified? This is the only thing I want to find out from you: did you receive the Spirit by the works of the Law, or by hearing with faith? Are you so foolish? Having begun by the Spirit, are you now being perfected by the flesh? Did you suffer so many things in vain—if indeed it was in vain? Does He then, who provides you with the Spirit and works miracles among you, do it by the works of the Law, or by hearing with faith? Even so Abraham believed God, and it was reckoned to him as righteousness. Therefore, be sure that it is those who are of faith who are sons of Abraham. And the Scripture, foreseeing that God would justify the Gentiles by faith, preached the gospel beforehand to Abraham, saying, "All the nations shall

be blessed in you." So then those who are of faith are blessed with Abraham, the believer.

Now can you see why denying the deity of Jesus Christ and the existence of the Holy Spirit invalidates Christianity? For if one denies Jesus' eternal divine nature and denies the existence of the Holy Spirit who seals the Christian until the day of redemption; as some do; then there is no Gospel or hope for the forgiveness of sin—as declared in Ephesians 1:13, 14 and 4:30; and in Jude 4. The book of Acts provides further history on the Gospel message and the growth of the church.

PROPHETICAL

Prophecies within the Scriptures are always accurate because they authenticate God's identity. Any prophecy given in the Scriptures that does not come true would make God a liar, thus ending God's claims to who he is—the true GOD!

Scholars may debate the number of prophecies in the bible, depending on how they see or interpret prophetic Scripture, with totals varying from 2,500—with 500 still to be fulfilled—to that reported by Wayne Jackson on Christincourier.com, who states that "J. Barton Payne's Encyclopedia of Biblical Prophecy lists 1,239 prophecies in the Old Testament and 578 prophecies in the New Testament, for a total of 1,817" [3] prophecies. In any case, the accuracy of the total number is less important than the accuracy of all the prophecies that have been identified.

The two categories of prophecies in scripture are Messianic—which focus on Jesus; and Non-messianic—which are about a wider range of events, nations, or individuals. The Old Testament contains just under half of the Bible's 700-plus messianic prophecies, and it should also be noted that some prophecies contain more than one projected fulfillment: one fulfillment coming in the lifetime of the prophet's hearers—to confirm the credibility of the prophet as God's messenger—and a second fulfillment to come at a future time. The first fulfillment enhanced the credibility of the second prophecy, even after the prophet had died. Christ himself demonstrated his role as a prophet, as Matthew 24:1-14 records for us here:

> And Jesus came out from the temple and was going away when His disciples came up to point out the temple buildings to Him. And He answered and said to them, do you not see all these things? Truly I say to you, not one stone here shall be left upon another, which will not be torn down.
>
> And as He was sitting on the Mount of Olives, the disciples came to Him privately, saying, "Tell us, when will these things be, and what will be the sign of Your coming, and of the end of the age?" And Jesus answered and said to them, "See to it that no one misleads you. For many will come in My name, saying, 'I am the Christ,' and will mislead many. And you will be hearing of wars and rumors of wars; see that you are not frightened, for those things must take place, but that is not yet the end. For nation will rise against nation, and kingdom against kingdom, and in various places there will be famines and earthquakes. But all these things are merely the beginning of birth pangs. Then they will deliver you to tribulation, and will kill you, and you will be hated by all nations on account of My name. And at that time many will fall away and will deliver up one another and hate one another. And many false prophets will arise, and will mislead many. And because lawlessness is increased, most people's love will grow cold. But the one who endures to the end, he shall be saved. And this gospel of the kingdom shall be preached in the whole world for a witness to all the nations, and then the end shall come.

THE GOSPEL FROM BEGINNING TO END

Just over forty years later, during the Jewish Rebellion of 70 A.D., the Romans killed many of the Jews living in Jerusalem and destroyed their temple. If you visit Israel today, all you will find of the temple is the outer Western Wall, which is sometimes called the "Wailing Wall." It was through the prophecy concerning the stones that Jesus' status as a prophet was confirmed. This prophecy validated Jesus as God's prophet to the people of his time because part of the prophecy came true within their lifetime. Other prophecies still to be fulfilled refer to the tribulation period that is mentioned in the books of Daniel and Revelation. If you would like to know why God allowed the destruction of the Jewish temple, for the second time in history, read Luke 19:41-44.

Some critics try to claim that many prophecies were written down after the events they predicted, even though Matthew was written between 58 and 68 A.D; and Mark, which recorded the same events Christ spoke to in Matthew 24, was written between 55 and 65 A.D.

To help gain some perspective on how accurate God's prophecies are, let us look at some messianic numbers. Old Testament Prophets predicted—up to a thousand years beforehand—many details of Jesus' coming: including the place, time and manner of his birth; how he would be betrayed; how he would die; how the people of his day would react to his presence; how his side would be pierced and how he would be buried. All of this came true—among many other things. Mathematicians have calculated that the likelihood of just eight of the many prophecies expressed in the Scriptures coming true about the same person, would be one in ten to the seventeenth power, or one in 100,000,000,000,000,000. You got it! One in one hundred quadrillion! For more information on this topic, you can lookup on-line Peter Stoner, Professor of Mathematics.

Isaiah 7:14 speaks about the virgin birth of Christ more than 700 years before it happened as recorded in Matthew

1:23. Isaiah 53:9-12 speaks of Christ being buried with the rich. Matthew 27:57-60 confirms that. Psalm 22:18 describes Christ's clothes being gambled over, or lots cast to see who would get them. Luke 23:34 confirms this taking place. Psalm 69:21 prophesied that gall and vinegar (wine) would be offered Christ as he hung on the Cross, and Matthew 27:34 confirms it. Psalm 22:1 quotes Jesus' dying words on the cross, which Matthew 27:46 confirms. Psalm 34:20 predicts that the coming Christ would not have any of his bones broken in his death, and John 19:36 testifies that no bones were broken. Zechariah 12:10 refers to the pierced side of Christ during his crucifixion. John 19:34 confirms that this took place. Psalm 16:10 prophesied that Christ would be raised from the dead; a fact confirmed by Mark 16:6-7. There are many more details like these and, as a matter of interest, the Psalms listed here were written between 1011 and 971 B.C., nearly 1,000 years before their fulfillment.[4]

You could spend a lifetime researching these facts and you are welcome to do so, but we need to move on to our next section: of eyewitnesses to the gospel message.

TESTIMONIAL

It should be remembered the Scriptures are not merely a collection of religious ideas, for there were many eyewitnesses to the life of Christ and the message of the gospel-promise. They are therefore recognized by literati, historians, archaeologists, philosophers, and theological scholars as historical documents to be read and studied for their valuable contribution in these specific areas of study. In addition, because the four Gospels provide us with the only detailed historical records of the life of Christ, we may accept them as valid. Moreover, one primary external source who corroborates the history of the early church is the Jewish historian Josephus, who lived from 37 until 100 A.D., and who witnessed the destruction of the temple in Jerusalem in 70 A.D.

As we walk through the Gospels, let us examine several testimonies about the identity of Jesus Christ. Firstly, from God's archangel Gabriel:

> Now in the sixth month the angel Gabriel was sent from God to a city in Galilee, called Nazareth, to a virgin engaged to a man whose name was Joseph, of the descendants of David; and the virgin's name was Mary. And coming in, he said to her, 'Hail, favored one! The Lord is with you.' But she was greatly troubled at this statement, and kept pondering what kind of salutation this might be. And the angel said to her, 'Do not be afraid, Mary; for you have found favor with God. And behold, you will conceive in your womb, and bear a son, and you shall name Him Jesus. He will be great, and will be called the Son of the Most High; and the Lord God will give Him the throne of His father David; and He will reign over the house of Jacob forever; and His kingdom will have no end.' And Mary said to the angel, 'How can this be, since I am a virgin?' And the angel answered and said to her, 'The Holy Spirit will come upon you, and the power of the Most High will overshadow you; and for that reason the holy offspring shall be called the Son of God. And behold, even your relative Elizabeth has also conceived a son in her old age; and she who was called barren is now in her sixth month. For nothing will be impossible with God.' And Mary said, 'Behold, the bondslave of the Lord; be it done to me according to your word.' And the angel departed from her. (Luke 1:26-38)

The next testimony comes in Matthew 3:13-17, from God the Father himself:

> Then Jesus arrived from Galilee at the Jordan coming to John, to be baptized by him. But John tried to prevent Him, saying, "I have need to be baptized by You, and do You come to me?" But Jesus answering said to him, "Permit it at this time; for in this way it is fitting for us to fulfil all righteousness." Then he permitted Him. And after being baptized, Jesus went up immediately from the water; and behold, the heavens were opened, and he saw the Spirit of God descending as a dove, and coming upon Him, and behold, a voice out of the heavens, saying, "This is My beloved Son, in whom I am well-pleased.

John the Baptist, who was born six months before Jesus, also recognizes him to be someone greater than himself, as shown in Luke 1:8-37 and John 1:29. On several occasions, demons recognized Jesus for who he was, with one of the most dramatic examples found in Matthew 8:28-32:

> And when He had come to the other side into the country of the Gadarenes, two men who were demon-possessed met Him as they were coming out of the tombs; they were so exceedingly violent that no one could pass by that road. And behold, they cried out, saying, "What do we have to do with You, Son of God? Have You come here to torment us before the time?" Now there was at a distance from them a herd of many swine feeding. And the demons began to entreat Him, saying, "If You are going to cast us out, send us into the herd of swine." And He said to them, "Begone!" And they came out, and went into the swine, and

behold, the whole herd rushed down the steep bank into the sea and perished in the waters.

When Jesus asked his disciples who they thought he was, it was Simon Peter who said, "'Thou art the Christ, the Son of the living God.' And Jesus answered and said to him, 'Blessed are you, Simon Barjona, because flesh and blood did not reveal this to you, but My Father who is in heaven.'" (Matthew 16:15-16)

Then we have the testimony of Jesus himself, in his conversation at a well with a Samaritan woman:

> Jesus said to her, "Woman, believe Me, an hour is coming when neither in this mountain, nor in Jerusalem, shall you worship the Father. You worship that which you do not know; we worship that which we know, for salvation is from the Jews. But an hour is coming, and now is, when the true worshipers shall worship the Father in spirit and truth; for such people the Father seeks to be His worshipers. God is spirit, and those who worship Him must worship in spirit and truth." The woman said to Him, "I know that Messiah is coming (He who is called Christ); when that One comes, He will declare all things to us." Jesus said to her, "I who speak to you am He." (John 4:21-26)

As Jesus died, the centurion, who was keeping guard over the area of the cross, made this observation as recorded in Matthew 27:50-54:

> And Jesus cried out again with a loud voice, and yielded up His spirit. And behold, the veil of the temple was torn in two from top to bottom, and the earth shook; and the rocks were split, and the tombs were opened; and many bodies of the saints who had fallen asleep were raised; and coming out of the tombs after His resurrection they entered the holy city

and appeared to many. Now the centurion, and those who were with him keeping guard over Jesus, when they saw the earthquake and the things that were happening, became very frightened and said, "Truly this was the Son of God!

This small sample of Gospel recognition of Jesus as the Christ; the Son of the living God; draws from differing sources, including representatives of the entire spirit world.

Perhaps the most powerful testimony about the truth of the Gospel message we could have is with Jesus himself. Consider the implications of this conversation he had with some Jewish leaders. "The Jews therefore gathered around Him, and were saying to Him, How long will You keep us in suspense? If You are the Christ, tell us plainly. Jesus answered them, I told you, and you do not believe; the works that I do in My Father's name, these bear witness of Me." (John 10:24-25) Yes, "the works that I do ... bear witness of Me." The works that he was referring to are recorded for us in the gospels. Remember Jesus' words to John the Baptist's disciples: "Go and report to John what you hear and see: the blind receive sight and the lame walk, the lepers are cleansed and the deaf hear, and the dead are raised up, and the poor have the gospel preached to them. And blessed is he who keeps from stumbling over Me." (Matthew 11:4-6)

The Gospel of John was written to bear witness that Jesus was the Christ, the Son of God; just as John concludes in his book as expressed here: "Many other signs therefore Jesus also performed in the presence of the disciples, which are not written in this book; but these have been written that you may believe that Jesus is the Christ, the Son of God; and that believing you may have life in His name." (John 20:30-31)

For this is the gospel, the good news that Jesus came to save that which was lost—meaning all of humanity.

THE GOSPEL FROM BEGINNING TO END

CHAPTER ENDNOTES

1. Answersingenesis.org, *How Long Did It Take for Noah to Build the Ark?*, available from https://answersingenesis.org/bible-timeline/how-long-did-it-take-for-noah-to-build-the-ark/; [database on line]; Internet; accessed 20 November 2014. (Link note was added as the source of information to the timeframe of building the ark.)

2. http://www.ancient-hebrew.org/11_language.html (Link note added for additional information for the reader.)

3. https://www.christiancourier.com/articles/318-how-many-prophecies-are-in-the-bible (Link add as a source of information.)

4. Reid A. Ashbaucher, *The Christian Faith: A Quick Guide to Understanding its Inter-Workings*, 2 ed. (Toledo: Reid Ashbaucher, 2017), 44.

Chapter 3

SOME HISTORICAL TEACHINGS OF THE CHRISTIAN FAITH

Teaching and doctrine are synonymous terms for Christian study of the faith as a whole, or in considering scriptural approaches to morality, relationships, and principal issues dealing with money, evaluation of self, personal responsibility, issues of sin, the plan of salvation, and the correct way to view God, the devil, and the world around us and how it all operates in everyday life.

This book seeks to offer an overview of the Christian faith, without trying to cover all of its doctrines in depth. You will find the following teaching to be essential for your understanding of basic Christianity, so you may grow in your knowledge of God the Father and the Lord Jesus Christ, without becoming confused or "swayed by every wind of doctrinal teaching," as Ephesians 4:11-16 warns us.

I will provide doctrinal concepts and their meanings from a Biblicist—or literal—perspective, while taking into account the legitimacy of Hebrew poetry and figurative language such as parables, allegories, similes, and metaphors. This type of interpretation, which also embraces cultural influences of biblical times, is also called the Grammatico—Historical Method.

For more in-depth information on this method, I recommend *The Interpretation of Prophecy*, by Paul Lee Tan, a Doctor of Theology and a leading authority on the discipline of the interpretation of biblical prophecy and biblical hermeneutics—which is the study of the "art and science of Scripture interpretation." (Out of print, but maybe available through TanBible.com.)

For those who are unfamiliar with American religious education degrees, the Th.D. or Doctor of Theology is the highest attainable academic degree, and it is mainly for teaching or for research. Many of its holders are college professors, college presidents or authors of religious or theological books; and it is only conferred after years of tertiary study: a four-year Bachelor of Arts course; another four years in gaining a Master of Theology (Th.M.), and four further years for the doctorate (Th.D.). Depending on the educational institution's requirements, candidates must complete a Master's thesis of between 80 and 250 pages, as well as a 125 to 350-page Doctrinal dissertation. They must also learn Hebrew and Greek plus two other foreign languages—usually chosen between Latin, Aramaic, French, and German. Most ministers or pastors earn a Master of Divinity degree (M.Div.), a three-year program after earning a four-year B.A. It includes writing a thesis and learning Hebrew and Greek. There are other paths to obtaining a Bible or Theology education, but these are the most prominent in relation to promoting leadership in the local church.

After all this education, one would expect to have a handle on the truth, but education does not produce truth. Truth only comes from one supreme source—God himself! The Holy Spirit perfectly teaches us biblical truth, as Jesus explains in John 14:25-26: "These things I have spoken to you, while abiding with you. But the Helper, the Holy Spirit, whom the Father will send in My name, He will teach you all things, and bring to your remembrance all that I said to you." The Scriptures confirm this in how Acts 4:13 describes the confusion of the religious leaders when the first Apostles confronted them. "Now as they observed the confidence of Peter and John, and understood that they were uneducated and untrained men, they were marvelling, and began to recognize them as having been with Jesus." In addition, just as these apostles experienced in their day, for today's Christian, the Holy Spirit still works in the same way.

SOME MAJOR DOCTRINES OF THE CHURCH

THE DOCTRINE OF GOD

Within the Scriptures, God is revealed as the self-existent one. That is, he needs nothing external of himself; he is eternally present, without beginning or ending. The Scriptures state it this way: "I am the Alpha and the Omega," says the Lord God, "who is and who was and who is to come, the Almighty." (Revelation 1:8) When he called Moses to lead Israel from slavery in Egypt, "God said to Moses, 'I AM WHO I AM'; Thus you shall say to the sons of Israel, I AM has sent me to you." (Exodus 3:14) And Romans 1:20 declares: "For since the creation of the world His invisible attributes, His eternal power, and divine nature, have been clearly seen, being understood through what has been made, so that they are without excuse." This means that creation—the natural universe—is a result of God's eternal power and nature and should be enough evidence to prove God's existence.

It is worth noting that during the 1,500 years that it took to compile the scriptures, none of the writers ever expresses the doubt of God's existence. Neither is there any mention of any atheists; though Psalm 14:1; 53:1 refer to unbelief: " The fool has said in his heart there is no God."

To help us understand who God is, the Scriptures describe attributes that are natural—that which focuses on his metaphysical aspects, and moral—that which deals with his personality. These attributes are equally applied to the Father, the Son, and the Holy Spirit, thus we have three persons unified with a single nature as reflected in these attributes.

NATURAL ATTRIBUTES

God is Spirit — John 4:24 "God is spirit, and those who worship Him must worship in spirit and truth." God has no physical body to be seen, but He communicates to us through His spirit, as First Corinthians 2:10-11 states: "For to us God revealed them through the Spirit; for the Spirit searches all things, even the depths of God. For who among men knows the thoughts of a man except the spirit of the man, which is in him? Even so the thoughts of God no one knows except the Spirit of God."

God is a Trinity — God did not reveal clearly, Trinitarianism (the concept of the trinity) in the Old Testament. However, the language of Genesis 1:26, 11:7, and Isaiah 48:12-16 infers that more than one person exists within God. In the New Testament God has chosen to reveal three persons comprising what theologians call the Godhead, as revealed in Matthew 3:16, 17; Matthew 28:19; Second Corinthians 13:14 and John 14:16. For the Scriptures declare: the Father is God in Romans 1:7; the Son is God in Hebrews 1:8 and the Holy Spirit is God in Acts 5:3, 4.

If you put these understandings together: God is spirit, and God is triune; the end result is that God is one spirit made up of three persons: God the Father, God the Son and God the Holy Spirit all existing as a single entity and sharing a single spirit nature which unifies the Godhead. For a more in-depth study on how to understand the trinity, I recommend my book called, *Made in the Image of God: Understanding the Nature of God and Mankind in a Changing World.* (Second Revised Edition)

God is Omniscient — All knowledge comes from God through His creation and His revelation, and as the author of knowledge, God is then all-knowing. Psalm 147:4-5 states: "He counts the number of the stars; He gives names to all of them. Great is our Lord, and abundant in strength; His understanding is infinite." How many stars are there in the universe? We do not even have a name for a number that goes that high—something to think about!

SOME HISTORICAL TEACHINGS OF THE CHRISTIAN FAITH

God is Omnipotent — Omnipotent means "all-mighty" or "all-powerful" with unlimited authority. The omnipotence of God simply means that God can bring to pass everything He wills to be so. While at the same time God has no one to oppose his actions and is free to do whatever He chooses to do within the limits of his own nature, meaning God only functions within the metaphysical makeup of His own nature. For example, God cannot lie (Leviticus 19:11; Titus 1:2), God cannot deny Himself (2 Timothy 2:13), God cannot be tempted by evil (James 1:13) and God cannot change his nature (Malachi 3:6). Consider the following discussion:

> The Lord said to Job, "Will the one who contends with the Almighty correct him? Let him who accuses God answer him!" Then Job answered the Lord: "I am unworthy—how can I reply to you? I put my hand over my mouth. I spoke once, but I have no answer—twice, but I will say no more." Then the Lord spoke to Job out of the storm: "Brace yourself like a man; I will question you, and you shall answer me. Would you discredit my justice? Would you condemn me to justify yourself? Do you have an arm like God's, and can your voice thunder like his? Then adorn yourself with glory and splendor, and clothe yourself in honor and majesty. Unleash the fury of your wrath, look at every proud man and bring him low, look at every proud man and humble him, crush the wicked where they stand. Bury them all in the dust together; shroud their faces in the grave. Then I myself will admit to you that your own right hand can save you." (Job 40:1-14: NIV)

God is Omnipresent — That is, God is present everywhere in spirit form. This is not to be confused with a spirit being like an angel or a ghost. God is spirit and his presence is all-encompassing, without limits or dimensions. To illustrate this in human terms, think of the earth's atmosphere, like the air that we breathe: it is everywhere we are, but existing as a single invisible element. Expand this idea into the entire universe as we know it. This analogy is drawn from Jesus' teaching found in John Chapter 3, connecting the concept of wind with the spirit world.

This doctrine should not be confused with Pantheism, which says God is everything, or in everything, but without personality. The Scriptures state in Psalm 139:7-10: "Where can I go from Thy Spirit? Or where can I flee from Thy presence? If I ascend to heaven, Thou art there; If I make my bed in Sheol, behold, Thou art there. If I take the wings of the dawn, If I dwell in the remotest part of the sea, Even there Thy hand will lead me, And Thy right hand will lay hold of me." And in Acts 7:48-50 we read, "However, the Most High does not dwell in houses made by human hands; as the prophet says: Heaven is My throne, And earth is the footstool of My feet; What kind of house will you build for Me? says the Lord; Or what place is there for My repose? Was it not My hand which made all these things?"

God is Eternal — That is; God is always present, without any past or future, and without a beginning or an end. God has declared for Himself to be the self-existent one as he expressed to Moses in Exodus 3:13-14: "Then Moses said to God, Behold, I am going to the sons of Israel, and I shall say to them, The God of your fathers has sent me to you. Now they may say to me, What is His name? What shall I say to them? And God said to Moses, 'I AM WHO I AM'; and He said, Thus you shall say to the sons of Israel, 'I AM has sent me to you.'"

Revelation 1:8 quotes God's declaration: "I am the Alpha and the Omega, says the Lord God, who is and who was and who is to come, the Almighty." Deuteronomy 33:27; Isaiah 9:6; Romans 16:26; Second Corinthians 4:18; First Peter 5:10 also affirms God as eternal.

SOME HISTORICAL TEACHINGS OF THE CHRISTIAN FAITH

God is Immutable — That is, God's nature never changes. Malachi 3:6 states: "For I, the LORD, do not change; therefore you, O sons of Jacob, are not consumed." This means no attributes listed hereunder both categories of "natural and moral" can be changed. God is all these things forever, and can never and will never change!

MORAL ATTRIBUTES

THE DOCTRINE OF GOD

God is Holy — God is without sin or corruption, and evil is not found in Him. God is perfect in all morality and is the standard for morality, for he hates sin and must turn away from it. Consider the following Scriptures: Leviticus 19:2: "Speak to all the congregation of the sons of Israel and say to them, 'You shall be holy, for I the LORD your God am holy.'" First Peter 1:15-16: "but like the Holy One who called you, be holy yourselves also in all your behavior; because it is written, 'You shall be holy, for I am holy.'" Proverbs 6:16-19: "There are six things which the Lord hates, Yes, seven which are an abomination to Him: Haughty eyes, a lying tongue, And hands that shed innocent blood, A heart that devises wicked plans, Feet that run rapidly to evil, A false witness who utters lies, And one who spreads strife among brothers."

God is Righteous — God is always in right standing, morally, within himself; because He is bound to maintain His holiness. There is no sin or any offense within the triune Godhead.
"The LORD is righteous in all His ways, and kind in all His deeds." (Psalm 145:17)

God is Merciful — Within his sovereignty—autonomous authority without limitations—God has the ability to display mercy to whomever He chooses. Romans 9:15 states: "For He says to Moses, 'I will have mercy on whom I have mercy, and I will have compassion on whom I have compassion.'"

God is All-Wise — God's wisdom and understanding are unlimited, for the Scriptures declare, "O Lord, how many are Thy works! In wisdom Thou hast made them all; the earth is full of Thy possessions." (Psalm 104:24) "For the Lord gives wisdom; From His mouth come knowledge and understanding." (Proverbs 2:6) "Great is our Lord, and abundant in strength; His understanding is infinite." (Psalm 147:5)

God is Love — Love is God's nature—not just compassionately but actively. The Scriptures express it this way: "For while we were still helpless, at the right time Christ died for the ungodly. For one will hardly die for a righteous man; though perhaps for the good man someone would dare even to die. But God demonstrates His own love toward us, in that while we were yet sinners, Christ died for us." (Romans 5:6-8) "For God so loved the world that He gave His only begotten Son, that whoever believes in Him should not perish, but have eternal life." (John 3:16) Another conversation about this subject can be found in First John Chapter 4.

THE DOCTRINE OF JESUS CHRIST

Jesus is God — That is, Jesus Christ was not created but shares the eternal unifying nature of God the Father and God the Holy Spirit. This is expressed in John 1:1-3, 14; 10:30; 20:30-31; and Titus 2:11-14.

Jesus is Man — That is, Jesus Christ was virgin born of Mary, who became the wife of Joseph, a direct descendant of King David; the descendant of Isaac; the descendant of Abraham; the descendant of

SOME HISTORICAL TEACHINGS OF THE CHRISTIAN FAITH

Shem; the descendant of Noah; the descendant of Seth; the descendant of Adam, the first man created by God. (Luke 3:23-38)

The virgin birth resulted from the Holy Spirit impregnating Mary before she had any sexual relations with her fiancé Joseph. After God told him in a dream how Mary became pregnant, Joseph then married her and had no sexual relations with her until she gave birth to Jesus. (Read: Isaiah 7:14; Matthew 1:18-25; Luke 1:26-38)

Because of the virgin birth, man's sin nature was never passed on to Jesus Christ; so Jesus was God in human form (incarnate). Therefore, by having human and divine natures, Jesus is fully God and fully Man. (Romans 1:1-4; Philippians 2:1-12)

Jesus is the Savior of the World — In Luke 2:10-11, the angel announces: "Do not be afraid; for behold, I bring you good news of a great joy which shall be for all the people; for today in the city of David there has been born for you a Savior, who is Christ the Lord." This salvation was enacted in Christ's crucifixion just outside Jerusalem's walls in a place called Calvary in Latin; the Skull in Greek; and Golgotha in Hebrew. This event was foretold in Isaiah 53:12; and described with explanations in Luke 23:33, John 3:16-17, 4:42, 19:17-37, First Peter 2:24-25, First Timothy 4:10 and First John 4:14.

THE DOCTRINE OF THE HOLY SPIRIT

The Person of the Holy Spirit is God — The Holy Spirit was not created, but shares in the eternal unifying nature of God the Father and God the Son. (See Romans 8:26-27; Mark 13:11; 1 Corinthians 2:13; Ephesians 4:30; Acts 16:6; John 14:16-17; 16:13-16; Isaiah 63:10-11.)

The Holy Spirit works in the world through his church or the body of Christ, through the permanent indwelling of each person that has participated by faith in the salvation process, or as Jesus put it in John 3, through being born again. The following list reflects how the Holy

Spirit works in his people and the world in particular through his body the church.

The Holy Spirit's Purpose:

- To bear witness that Jesus is the Christ, the eternal incarnate Son of God. (John 16:13-14)

- To baptize the believer (which fulfills the New Covenant). (Acts 1:5; Jeremiah 31:31-34)

- To empower the believer, providing believers the ability to carry out God's purposes. (Acts 1:8)

- To guide the believer in the direction God desires them to go. (Acts 10:19; 13:14; 16:6; 21:11)

- To provide spiritual gifting, used for service to others. (1 Corinthians 12)

- To provide God's wisdom for understanding God's truth. (1 Corinthians 12:8)

- To bring assurance of the believer's salvation. (Hebrews 10:15; Romans 8:16; John 14:16)

- To seal the believer, guaranteeing eternal life. (2 Corinthians 1:22; Ephesians 1:13; 4:30)

- To convict the world of sin. (John 16:7-11)

SOME HISTORICAL TEACHINGS OF THE CHRISTIAN FAITH

- To teach the believer according to God's words. (John 14:26)

- To bring an understanding of God and his ways to the believer. (1 Corinthians 2:10-16)

THE DOCTRINE OF HUMANKIND

God created humanity in his image, perfect in every way, to walk with, to worship, and to have fellowship with God (Genesis 1:26-27; 2:18-24). However, humanity, tempted by evil through the deceit of the devil called Satan, made a willful choice to disobey God's commandment. According to God's word, through one rebellious act, human nature became corrupt with sin and our nature has become like Satan's nature, full of pride, lust, and selfishness. This sinful choice separated us from God (Genesis 3:1-17; Romans 3:23; Mark 7:21-23; 1 John 2:16; John 8:44; Romans 3:9-18).

THE DOCTRINE OF SALVATION

Because humanity has fallen into a sinful state, it is now under the judgment of God, who requires a penalty to be paid—which is death. (Romans 3:23; John 3:18-19; Romans 3:9-18; Revelation 20:11-15)

Yet because of God's love for his creation, he has provided a plan of salvation for humankind to escape God's own judgment. This is why the Scriptures state that salvation is from the Lord! (Psalm 3:8; 37:39-40; John 2:9; 3:16)

God's salvation plan is a work of grace, which means to show mercy or kindness towards someone. Grace is simply an act of mercy or kindness towards those who are in your debt and deserve no favors. Jesus' parable from Matthew 18:23-35 illustrates this grace as expressed here:

CHRISTIANITY 101

For this reason the kingdom of heaven may be compared to a certain king who wished to settle accounts with his slaves. And when he had begun to settle them, there was brought to him one who owed him ten thousand talents. But since he did not have the means to repay, his lord commanded him to be sold, along with his wife and children and all that he had, and repayment to be made. The slave therefore falling down, prostrated himself before him, saying, 'Have patience with me, and I will repay you everything.' And the lord of that slave felt compassion and released him and forgave him the debt. But that slave went out and found one of his fellow slaves who owed him a hundred denarii; and he seized him and began to choke him, saying, 'Pay back what you owe.' So his fellow slave fell down and began to entreat him, saying, 'Have patience with me and I will repay you.' He was unwilling however, but went and threw him in prison until he should pay back what was owed. So when his fellow slaves saw what had happened, they were deeply grieved and came and reported to their lord all that had happened. Then summoning him, his lord said to him, 'You wicked slave, I forgave you all that debt because you entreated me. Should you not also have had mercy on your fellow slave, even as I had mercy on you?' And his lord, moved with anger, handed him over to the torturers until he should repay all that was owed him. So shall My heavenly Father also do to you, if each of you does not forgive his brother from your heart.

God offers salvation to the world by his grace, as the only way to escape his judgment. Jesus Christ, God's only Son, came in human form to die in humanity's place as payment for its sins, an action that is called the "atonement," an "offering of restitution" for being guilty of offenses committed and describes the sacrificial death of Christ for the restitution of humanity with God. The atonement is rooted in the Old Testament sacrificial practices (Exodus 30:10), but its eternal fulfillment, by God's design, came through Jesus' final sacrifice on a Roman cross. (Read, Romans 5 [KJV] and the book of Hebrews.)

The requirements to receive salvation are repentance and faith, as Jesus stated in Mark 1:15: "The time is fulfilled, and the kingdom of God is at hand; repent and believe in the gospel." Jesus emphasized faith many times as he healed people: "Your faith has saved you; go in peace." (Luke 7:50) As Paul testified: "I did not shrink from declaring to you anything that was profitable, and teaching you publicly and from house to house, solemnly testifying to both Jews and Greeks of repentance toward God and faith in our Lord Jesus Christ." (Acts 20:20-21) Hebrews 11:6 also says, "And without faith it is impossible to please Him, for he who comes to God must believe that He is, and that He is a rewarder of those who seek Him."

To summarize; salvation is not a reward for being or doing good, but a gift which we claim by faith, as the Apostle Paul stated, "For by grace you have been saved through faith; and that not of yourselves, it is the gift of God; not as a result of works, that no one should boast." (Ephesians 2:8-9) If our good works could save us, then we would be able to boast in heaven on what we did, thus making Jesus' sacrifice worthless. As Paul also explained to the Galatians:

> ... know that a man is not justified by observing the law, but by faith in Jesus Christ. So we, too, have put our faith in Christ Jesus that we may be justified by faith in Christ and not by observing the law, because by observing the law no one will be justified. If, while we seek to be justified in Christ, it becomes evident that we ourselves are sinners, does that mean that Christ promotes sin? Absolutely not! If I rebuild what I destroyed, I prove that I am a lawbreaker. For through the law I died to the law so that I might live for God. I have

been crucified with Christ and I no longer live, but Christ lives in me. The life I live in the body, I live by faith in the Son of God, who loved me and gave himself for me. I do not set aside the grace of God, for if righteousness could be gained through the law, Christ died for nothing! (Galatians 2:16-21; NIV)

So how does one become part of the Christian faith? By simply repenting and confessing your sins to God and accepting the death, burial, and bodily resurrection of Jesus Christ, as payment for your sins before God. Therefore, by faith in Christ's work on the cross alone, your sins are forgiven. For the Scripture says: "... if you confess with your mouth (that) Jesus is Lord, and believe in your heart that God raised him from the dead, you will be saved. For it is with your heart that you believe and are justified, and it is with your mouth that you confess and are saved." (Romans 10:9; NIV)

The Scriptures also express how wide God's offer of salvation is: "The Lord is not slow about His promise, as some count slowness, but is patient toward you, not wishing for any to perish but for all to come to repentance," (2 Peter 3:9) and, "Anyone who trusts in him will never be put to shame. For there is no difference between Jew and Gentile—the same Lord is Lord of all and richly blesses all who call on him, for, Everyone who calls on the name of the Lord will be saved." (Romans 10:11-13; NIV)

If you would like to know more about Jesus Christ and his plan for the salvation of his creation, I recommend reading the Gospel of John, the fourth book of the New Testament.

THE DOCTRINE OF THE SCRIPTURES

The Scriptures make four claims about themselves and are listed as follows:

SOME HISTORICAL TEACHINGS OF THE CHRISTIAN FAITH

The Claim to be True

- Psalm 119:160 — "The sum of Thy word is truth, and every one of Thy righteous ordinances is everlasting." (A statement made in the Old Testament.)

- John 17:17 — "Sanctify them in the truth; Thy word is truth." (Jesus' prayer in the New Testament.)

The Claim to be Inspired by God

- Second Timothy 3:16,17 states: "All Scripture is inspired by God and profitable for teaching, for reproof, for correction, for training in righteousness; that the man of God may be adequate, equipped for every good work."

- Second Peter 1:12-21 states:

"Therefore, I shall always be ready to remind you of these things, even though you already know them, and have been established in the truth which is present with you. And I consider it right, as long as I am in this earthly dwelling, to stir you up by way of reminder, knowing that the laying aside of my earthly dwelling is imminent, as also our Lord Jesus Christ has made clear to me. And I will also be diligent that at any time after my departure you may be able to call these things to mind. For we did not follow cleverly devised tales when we made known to you the power and coming of our Lord Jesus Christ, but we were eyewitnesses of His majesty. For when He received honor and glory from God the Father, such an utterance as this was made to Him by the Majestic Glory, 'This is My beloved Son with whom I am well-pleased'—and we ourselves heard this utterance made from heaven when we were with Him on the holy mountain. And so we have the prophetic word made more sure, to which you do well to pay attention as to a lamp shining in a dark place, until the day dawns and the morning star arises in your hearts. But know this first of all, that no prophecy of Scripture is a matter of one's own interpretation, for no prophecy was ever made by an act of human will, but men moved by the Holy Spirit spoke from God."

The Claim to be Eternal

- Matthew 5:18, 19 — "For truly I say to you, until heaven and earth pass away, not the smallest letter or stroke shall pass away from the Law, until all is accomplished. Whoever then annuls one of the least of these commandments, and so teaches others, shall be called least in the kingdom of heaven; but whoever keeps and teaches them, he shall be called great in the kingdom of heaven."

- Matthew 24:35 — "Heaven and earth will pass away, but My words shall not pass away."

- Hebrews 11:3 — "By faith we understand that the worlds were prepared by the word of God, so that what is seen was not made out of things which are visible."

The Claim that Jesus Christ is the "Word of God" in the Flesh— Fulfilling all the Scriptures

- John 1:1-5, 14 — "In the beginning was the Word, and the Word was with God, and the Word was God. He was in the beginning with God. All things came into being by Him, and apart from Him nothing came into being that has come into being. In Him was life, and the life was the light of men. And the light shines in the darkness, and the darkness did not comprehend it." (vs.14) "And the Word became flesh, and dwelt among us, and we beheld His glory, glory as of the only begotten from the Father, full of grace and truth."

- Matthew 5:17, 18 — "Do not think that I came to abolish the Law or the Prophets; I did not come to abolish, but to fulfil. For truly I say to you, until heaven and earth pass away, not the smallest letter or stroke shall pass away from the Law, until all is accomplished."

- Luke 24:27 — "And beginning with Moses and with all the prophets, He explained to them the things concerning Himself in all the Scriptures."

These Scriptures and many others, affirm the Protestant Christian church's claim that the original Scriptures are divinely inspired: that they are verbal—documented and written; plenary—complete in every way; and inerrant—without errors. While some would claim the English Scriptures to be 100% error-free, others would allow for the fallibility of copying errors or translation difficulties, which will be discussed in another chapter.

CHRISTIANITY 101

THE DOCTRINE ON THE CHURCH

First Century History

The book of Acts relates how the Church started and progressed in the first century, though Jesus also mentions the church during his ministry, as recorded in Matthew 16:13-18:

> Now when Jesus came into the district of Caesarea Philippi, He began asking His disciples, saying, 'Who do people say that the Son of Man is?' And they said, 'Some say John the Baptist; and others, Elijah; but still others, Jeremiah, or one of the prophets.' He said to them, 'But who do you say that I am?' And Simon Peter answered and said, 'Thou art the Christ, the Son of the living God.' And Jesus answered and said to him, 'Blessed are you, Simon Barjona, because flesh and blood did not reveal this to you, but My Father who is in heaven. And I also say to you that you are Peter, and upon this rock I will build My church; and the gates of Hades shall not overpower it.'

Some interpret Jesus' phrase "this rock" as referring to Peter, and hold long discussions on the meaning of Peter's name (little stone or rock) and the lack of capitalization of the word "rock." It is my view the word "rock" is referring to Christ. Why do I believe this? Because God's plan was never intended for Christ to build his church on fallible human beings, for the Scriptures refer to Christ as the chief cornerstone from all biblical teaching, as the following Scriptures show:

- Psalm 118:22, 23 — "The stone which the builders rejected has become the chief cornerstone. This is the Lord's doing; It is marvellous in our eyes."

SOME HISTORICAL TEACHINGS OF THE CHRISTIAN FAITH

- Isaiah 28:16 — "Therefore thus says the Lord God, Behold, I am laying in Zion a stone, a tested stone, a costly corner stone for the foundation, firmly placed. He who believes in it will not be disturbed."

- Acts 4:10,11,12 — "... let it be known to all of you, and to all the people of Israel, that by the name of Jesus Christ the Nazarene, whom you crucified, whom God raised from the dead—by this name this man stands here before you in good health. He is the stone which was rejected by you, the builders, but which became the very corner stone. And there is salvation in no one else; for there is no other name under heaven that has been given among men, by which we must be saved."

- First Corinthians 3:11 — "For no man can lay a foundation other than the one which is laid, which is Jesus Christ."

- Ephesians 2:19, 20, 21, 22 — "So then you are no longer strangers and aliens, but you are fellow citizens with the saints, and are of God's household, having been built upon the foundation of the apostles and prophets, Christ Jesus Himself being the corner stone, in whom the whole building, being fitted together is growing into a holy temple in the Lord; in whom you also are being built together into a dwelling of God in the Spirit."

The two Old Testament Scripture passages listed above predicted the reaction of Israel's leadership when Christ came: rejecting him as the promised Messiah (Savior). Matthew 21:33-46, Mark 12:1-12, Luke 20:9-20, First Peter 2:1-8 all provide details of their opposition to him as the chief cornerstone, a symbol representing Christ himself, as the starting point and foundation to build true faith in God.

Some believe that the Jewish rejection of Christ means that the church became a spiritual replacement of the Nation Israel as represented in the Old Testament; and God is no longer dealing with them as his chosen people. This view comes through a mistaken interpretation of the word "church," represented solely to mean a "congregation or assembly," and how one views the covenants; I will talk more on this topic in another chapter.

A scriptural review of this subject of replacement reveals a different picture. The key is found in the concept of "mysteries;" which are foundational concepts that God purposely concealed in the Old Testament—to be fully revealed through the teachings of the New Testament. The Apostle Paul begins to reveal this in Ephesians 5:32 when he says, "This mystery is great; but I am speaking with reference to Christ and the church." Both Christ and the Church are presented to us in the New Testament as mysteries and this is how they are presented.

God chose the Jewish people, or the Old Testament nation of Israel, through his everlasting covenant made with Abraham, Isaac, and Jacob. Genesis 12:3 states that as part of this covenant, all nations will be blessed. This blessing is confirmed to us in Galatians 3:8, which states the Gospel of Jesus Christ is the source of this blessing. For this blessing to take effect, three mysteries must be revealed: the mystery of Christ, the mystery of the Holy Spirit, and the mystery of the Church. Let us look at these for a better understanding.

The Mystery of Christ

The mystery of Christ revealed to us starts in Colossians 1:25-27: "Of this church I was made a minister according to the stewardship from God bestowed on me for your benefit, that I might fully carry out the preaching of the word of God, that is, the mystery which has been hidden from the past ages and generations; but has now been manifested to His saints, to whom God willed to make known what is the riches of the glory of this mystery among the Gentiles, which is Christ in you, the hope of glory." The mystery revealed is "Christ in you, the hope of glory," of which Paul also wrote about in Ephesians 3:1-8:

> For this reason I, Paul, the prisoner of Christ Jesus for the sake of you Gentiles — if indeed you have heard of the stewardship of God's grace which was given to me for you; that by revelation there was made known to me the mystery, as I wrote before in brief. And by referring to this, when you read you can understand my insight into the mystery of Christ, which in other generations was not made known to the sons of men, as it has now been revealed to His holy apostles and prophets in the Spirit; to be specific, that the Gentiles are fellow heirs and fellow members of the body, and fellow partakers of the promise in Christ Jesus through the gospel, of which I was made a minister, according to the gift of God's grace which was given to me according to the working of His power.

Therefore, through the mystery of Christ, God now offers salvation to Gentiles (non-Jews) as well as to the Jews; not to replace them, but as a temporary bypass, as explained to us in Romans 11:11 which states: "I say then, they did not stumble so as to fall, did they? May it never be! But by their transgression salvation has come to the Gentiles, to make them jealous." The Apostle Paul further explains this to us in Romans 11:25-32 as expressed here:

> For I do not want you, brethren, to be uninformed of this mystery, lest you be wise in your own estimation, that a

partial hardening has happened to Israel until the fullness of the Gentiles has come in; and thus

> *all Israel will be saved; just as it is written,*
> *The Deliverer will come from Zion,*
> *He will remove ungodliness from Jacob.*
> *And this is My covenant with them,*
> *When I take away their sins.*

From the standpoint of the gospel they are enemies for your sake, but from the standpoint of God's choice they are beloved for the sake of the fathers; for the gifts and the calling of God are irrevocable. For just as you once were disobedient to God, but now have been shown mercy because of their disobedience, so these also now have been disobedient, in order that because of the mercy shown to you they also may now be shown mercy. For God has shut up all in disobedience that He might show mercy to all.

God bypassed Israel to extend salvation to the Gentiles, but will re-establish Israel as a nation and his chosen people again; "for the gifts and the calling of God are irrevocable." (Romans 11:29; John 10:16; Isaiah 56:8) For the full context of this mystery, I recommend you read Romans Chapter 11.

Many Christians, including myself, believe that Israel's restoration began in 1948 when Israel was legally recognized by the world to be an independent, sovereign, and free Jewish Nation.

The Mystery of the Church

Romans 11:25's phrase, "until the fullness of the Gentiles has come in," is mostly interpreted to mean the "Church Age," or until Christ finishes building his universal church, instead of the nation of

Israel. Many also believe this "Church Age" will come to an end when Jesus returns in the sky to take or rapture (a theological term) his Church to be with him forever, though not all Christians hold to this particular view, therefore for better continuity to our discussion we will cover this topic in another chapter. As to our original discussion, the mystery of the church is revealed as seen in Ephesians 3:4-13:

> And by referring to this, when you read you can understand my insight into the mystery of Christ, which in other generations was not made known to the sons of men, as it has now been revealed to His holy apostles and prophets in the Spirit; to be specific, that the Gentiles are fellow heirs and fellow members of the body, and fellow partakers of the promise in Christ Jesus through the gospel, of which I was made a minister, according to the gift of God's grace which was given to me according to the working of His power. To me, the very least of all saints, this grace was given, to preach to the Gentiles the unfathomable riches of Christ, and to bring to light what is the administration of the mystery which for ages has been hidden in God, who created all things; in order that the manifold wisdom of God might now be made known through the church to the rulers and the authorities in the heavenly places. This was in accordance with the eternal purpose which He carried out in Christ Jesus our Lord, in whom we have boldness and confident access through faith in Him. Therefore I ask you not to lose heart at my tribulations on your behalf, for they are your glory.

That "God might now be made known through the church"—as stated above—is one purpose of the church; with First Timothy 3:14-15 defining the Church's other purpose as expressed here: "I am writing these things to you, hoping to come to you before long; but in case I am delayed, I write so that you may know how one ought to conduct himself in the household of God, which is the church of the living God, the pillar and support of the truth." Yes, not only is the church the human means of spreading the Gospel, but the church is also to be the pillar and support of the truth. And what truth is the church supporting? The Word of God! The Holy Scriptures! This can be seen in Psalm 119:60 and John 17:17 where Jesus says, "Sanctify them in the truth; Thy word is truth."

The Mystery of the Holy Spirit

Our final mystery to be revealed is the person of the Holy Spirit. Why is this important? Because without the Holy Spirit the new covenant could never be fulfilled! The mystery of "Christ in you," comes through the work of the Holy Spirit. Remember what the new covenant states in Jeremiah 31:33-34? "But this is the covenant which I will make with the house of Israel after those days, declares the Lord, I will put My law within them, and on their heart I will write it; and I will be their God, and they shall be My people. And they shall not teach again, each man his neighbor and each man his brother, saying, 'Know the Lord,' for they shall all know Me, from the least of them to the greatest of them, declares the Lord, for I will forgive their iniquity, and their sin I will remember no more."

God puts his law in human hearts and teaches us through his indwelling Holy Spirit; as Jesus explains in John 14:16-17: "And I will ask the Father, and He will give you another Helper, that He may be with you forever; that is the Spirit of truth, whom the world cannot receive, because it does not behold Him or know Him, but you know Him because He abides with you, and will be in you." He reinforces this promise in verses 25-26 which reads: "These things I have spoken to you, while abiding with you. But the Helper, the Holy Spirit, whom the Father will send in My name, He will teach you all things, and bring to your remembrance all that I said to you." Later, in John 16:13-14, he adds: "But when He, the Spirit of truth, comes, He will guide you into all the truth; for He will not speak on His own initiative, but whatever He hears, He will speak; and He will disclose to you what is to come. He shall glorify Me; for He shall take of Mine, and shall disclose it to you."

Thus Jesus reveals to us the person of the Holy Spirit; a mystery from times past; for throughout the Old Testament, Israel only knew God as one God, as expressed in Deuteronomy 6:4: "Hear, O Israel! The Lord is our God, the Lord is one!" This does not reflect a trinity or a three in one concept. Mark 12:28-34 bears this Old Testament teaching out as we read:

> And one of the scribes came and heard them arguing, and recognizing that He had answered them well, asked Him, What commandment is the foremost of all? Jesus answered, 'The foremost is, Hear, O Israel! The Lord our God is one Lord; and you shall love the Lord your God with all your heart, and with all your soul, and with all your mind, and with all your strength. The second is this, shall love your neighbor as yourself. There is no other commandment greater than these.' And the scribe said to Him, Right, Teacher, You have truly stated that He is One; and there is no one else besides Him; and to love Him with all the heart and with all the understanding and with all the strength, and to love one's neighbor as himself, is much more than all burnt offerings and sacrifices. And when Jesus saw that he had answered intelligently, He said to him, You are not far from the kingdom of God. And after that, no one would venture to ask Him any more questions.

So you can see, not until Jesus Christ's coming, is the world introduced to the third person of the Godhead—the person of the Holy Spirit. As you read through the New Testament, you will begin to understand the importance of the person and work of the Holy Spirit, but it should be remembered the purpose of the Holy Spirit is not to bring honor and glory to Himself, but to point the world to the person and work of Jesus Christ—"the hope of glory." This is sometimes why the Holy Spirit is referred to in theology as the silent partner because he never makes reference or refers to himself.

UNDERSTANDING THE CONCEPT OF A UNIVERSAL CHURCH

The New Testament defines the church as the "Body of Christ," with Christ as the head: providing life, authority, direction and purpose. The "Body of Christ" refers to believers in Christ Jesus worldwide, who are born-again, through faith alone, as expressed in John 3:1-18. Another theological term for the church is the "bride of Christ," (Ephesians 5:32) with believers being spiritually married to Christ the bridegroom. There is only one "body" or "bride"; terms which embrace a single universal church; as affirmed by Romans 7:1-4; Ephesians 4:9:13; 5:1-33; Colossians 1:15-29; Hebrews 12:22-24; First Corinthians 10:14-17; John 3:1-15; 27-29 and Matthew 9:15.

UNDERSTANDING THE CONCEPT OF A LOCAL NEW TESTAMENT CHURCH

The New Testament refers to local congregations of churches of different sizes. They also met in different places: some in homes, others outdoors or in buildings, and—when the Roman persecution began—in hiding, all reflected in Acts 8:1-2; 9:31; 13:1; Romans 16:1-5; First Corinthians 1:2; and Revelation Chapters 2 and 3.

SOME HISTORICAL TEACHINGS OF THE CHRISTIAN FAITH

From the beginning, the church was guided and taught by the Apostles, whose authority came via the Holy Spirit. As the church began to spread to other parts of the world, the Apostles gave instructions regarding its organization, leadership, sound teaching, discipline according to Christ's commandments, and the sacraments of baptism and the Lord's Supper—also described or referred to as The Lord's Table or Communion by today's church.

OFFICES OF THE CHURCH

THE OFFICE OF ELDER, PASTOR, BISHOP, AND OVERSEER

The offices of the church are named Elder, Pastor, Bishop, Overseer, and Deacon. (1 Peter 5:1-5; 1 Timothy 3, KJV; Ephesians 4:11; Philippians 1:1; Titus 1:5)

These titles, except for Deacon, are sometimes interpreted differently within local churches, according to a variety of spiritual speaking gifts given them by the Holy Spirit. But it is my view that biblically they share equal spiritual authority (Ephesians 4:11). The speaking gifts the Scriptures reference are, Teacher, Pastor, Evangelist, and Prophet, though some local churches believe the gifts of prophecy and of speaking in tongues no longer exists. This is a matter of interpretation, for it is my view that all spiritual gifts still exist in some form; but this is a completely different discussion, which I will leave as a further topic for you to study. Individual Christians may also be given gifts of wisdom, leadership, administration, and the gift of helps and service. There are other spiritual gifts given by the Holy Spirit, with at least one and sometimes more are given to every Christian at salvation, which should be used to help and build up or encourage other believers who make up the body of Christ—the church (1 Corinthians 12:1-11; 14:1-19; Hebrews 2:4; Romans 12:4-8).

THE OFFICE OF DEACON

Deacon is another office: a position of service to others in the body of Christ. They were helpers to the Elders, who focused on studying and teaching, and dealing with the spiritual needs of the church; while deacons took care of practical or physical issues, handling everyday needs of the church, such as the needs of widows, among other things. Women who held this office were called deaconesses (1 Timothy 3:10, Romans 16:1; RSV).

First Timothy and Titus list spiritual qualifications for all leadership, both male and female.

From these principles and practices, today's churches have tried to model their forms of church government, these forms vary with every church, so I will try to cover the basics on this issue when we consider church polity in another chapter.

ORDINANCES OF THE CHURCH

THE LORD'S SUPPER OR COMMUNION

Jesus, as a memorial to symbolize his imminent sacrificial death for the forgiveness of sins, instituted the Lord's Supper, replacing the Jewish Passover. The Lord's Supper is observed as a memorial of His death, burial, and resurrection even to this day by all Christian churches. (See Matthew 26:17-30)

The Lord's Supper's roots are in the Jewish Passover, whose detailed instructions are recorded in Exodus 12:1-14; as "a memorial to you, and you shall celebrate it as a feast to the LORD; throughout your generations you are to celebrate it as a permanent ordinance." This Jewish celebration feast commemorates God's saving Israel from 400 years of slavery in Egypt.

Jesus established the Lord's Supper to replace the Passover upon His death, just as the new covenant fulfilled and replaced the old covenant made with Moses. For he said in Matthew 5:17, "Do not think that I came to abolish the Law or the Prophets; I did not come to abolish, but to fulfil." At his death, the new covenant was put in place along with the Lord's Supper. The slavery of Israel to Egypt, and the memorial of the Passover to remember God's deliverance from that slavery, is seen as the foreshadowing of Jesus' death and resurrection for the deliverance of His people from their bondage to sin. (See Romans 7:14 and Galatians 4:3-5)

The implementation of the Lord's Supper is described in detail in First Corinthians 11:20-34, and it is much simpler than the Passover—requiring no animal blood sacrifice because Christ became the permanent blood sacrifice. (See Isaiah 53:7, John 1:36 and 1 Peter 1:19)

Unlike the annual Passover, the Lord's Supper can be observed whenever the Christian community chooses. However, like the Passover, the Lord's Supper came with a warning attached. (See First Corinthians 11:27-34)

The Lord's Supper is observed by the worldwide church, though each church interprets it differently. Catholics believe in transubstantiation: that the bread and wine at some point in the observance literally turn into the blood and the body of Christ himself. Some Protestant groups believe in Consubstantiation: that Christ is somehow physically present and part of the event. Many other churches view the Lord's Supper as strictly a symbolic event, and one of two ordinances of the church, with baptism being the second.

Those churches that hold a more symbolic view of the Lord's Supper usually substitute the wine with some other drink made from grapes (non-alcoholic) to avoid being an obstacle to other believers. For someone that is saved from alcoholism, serving an alcoholic wine could be a problem or stumbling block to that person; and there are those in the body of Christ that abstain from alcohol, as a matter of conscience, based on a personal understanding of their faith.

Summarizing this segment, the Lord's Supper is simply a memorial service remembering the life of Christ, his sacrificial death, burial and resurrection that resulted in the creation of the church or body of Christ, in which he purchased with His blood for the remissions of sin (Acts 20:28).

BAPTISM

Baptism is understood according to one's theological teaching or training, with the Greek verb form of the word "baptizo" meaning to immerse or submerge. Biblically, baptism's firstly refers to the ministry of John the Baptist. (See Matthew 3:4-9) Through Jesus' example, baptism seemed to be performed by immersing or submerging a person underwater. (See Matthew 3:16)

The biblical purpose of baptism is debated among the Christian community according to how one interprets the doctrine of Salvation. Out of 159 references to the word salvation in the English Scriptures, there are no references to a baptism of any kind. Major biblical statements about salvation are seen in the following Scriptures:

- Acts 4:12 — "And there is salvation in no one else; for there is no other name under heaven that has been given among men, by which we must be saved."

- Romans 10:8-13 — "But what does it say? The word is near you, in your mouth and in your heart—that is, the word of faith which we are preaching, that if you confess with your mouth Jesus as Lord, and believe in your heart that God raised Him from the dead, you shall be saved; for with the heart man believes, resulting in righteousness, and with the mouth he confesses, resulting in salvation. For the Scripture says, Whoever believes in Him will not be disappointed. For there is no distinction between Jew and

Greek; for the same Lord is Lord of all, abounding in riches for all who call upon Him; for Whoever will call upon the name of the Lord will be saved."

- 2 Corinthians 7:9 — "For the sorrow that is according to the will of God produces a repentance without regret, leading to salvation; but the sorrow of the world produces death."

- Hebrews 11:7 — "By faith Noah, being warned by God about things not yet seen, in reverence prepared an ark for the salvation of his household, by which he condemned the world, and became an heir of the righteousness which is according to faith."

When examining the word "saved," we find it listed in the English Scriptures 90 times. Of those 90 listings, only three of them mention baptism (See Mark 16:16, Acts 2:40; 16:30-33). Based on these three Scriptures, some Christians insist that baptism is required for salvation to be complete; though a simple explanation could be offered by distinguishing the difference between "John the Baptist baptism" and Jesus' "baptism of the Holy Spirit." John's baptism was for repentance, in preparation for the imminent arrival of the Messiah Jesus, as John declared in Mark 1:8, "I baptized you with water; but He will baptize you with the Holy Spirit." The baptism of the Holy Spirit takes place at the moment of salvation and is a permanent indwelling of the Holy Spirit as promised in the New Covenant and referred to in Jeremiah 31:31-34. With Acts being a transitional book from the Old Testament practices of Judaism to the New Testament's new way of life through Christ as reflected in Christianity, the need to distinguish the difference between John's baptism and Christ's baptism of the Holy Spirit meant that people were instructed in Acts to be saved and baptized, to make the point that there was a difference between the two types of baptisms. This transition process is best illustrated for us in Acts 11:12-18.

By looking at the following Scriptures, we can begin to understand how this explanation fits the Acts 11 scenario. Mark 16:15-16 Jesus said, "He who has believed and has been baptized shall be saved; but he who has disbelieved shall be condemned." He did not say that if you were not baptized you would be condemned, only if you did not believe. Similarly, in Luke 7:50, "He said to the woman, Your faith has saved you; go in peace;" A statement that includes no instruction to be baptized at all. In Matthew 28:18-20, Jesus Great Commission reads, "All authority has been given to Me in heaven and on earth. Go therefore and make disciples of all the nations, baptizing them in the name of the Father and the Son and the Holy Spirit, teaching them to observe all that I commanded you; and lo, I am with you always, even to the end of the age." These verses indicate that making disciples represents the salvation of humanity, with baptism representing identification or affiliation with being a disciple of Christ the Savior. This seems to align with Jesus' words in Matthew 10:32-33: "Everyone therefore who shall confess Me before men, I will also confess him before My Father who is in heaven. But whoever shall deny Me before men, I will also deny him before My Father who is in heaven." Thus, baptism is a public confession that one is a follower of Jesus Christ.

Some would view that to require baptism to complete the salvation process, is to require works to become part of this experience; when Galatians 2:16, 17 expressly reject works as part of the salvation experience, this is something to think about!

OTHER ISSUES OF BAPTISM

Churches have different methods of baptism. Some sprinkle waters on the head, others dip part of the body underwater and others immerse the whole body underwater. It is the view of some Protestant churches and the vast majority of Baptist churches that total submergence is the scriptural method of baptism.

The Scriptures teach that only believers in Christ should be baptized. This doctrine is called "believer's baptism," and requires sufficient maturity of the candidates to understand the Gospel message and the concept of sin. This may vary with each individual, for I have heard testimonies of people as young as four years old making this commitment. But it is certain, that infants, babies under two, are not capable of such decisions and should not be baptized for the intended purpose of scriptural baptism.

Water baptism is a public expression of a person's desire to be a follower of Jesus Christ. Going under the water symbolizes burial with Christ and coming out of the water symbolizes being raised from that death into eternal life with Christ. The words used at baptisms should always identify the authority in which the baptism is being performed: in the name of God the Father, God the Son, and God the Holy Spirit. This is by commandment as found in Matthew 28:18-20.

As expressed before, baptism of the Holy Spirit takes place at the time of one's conversion, when someone repents of their sins and accepts Jesus Christ as their personal Savior from God's judgment. At that moment, the Holy Spirit enters the believer in a real and physical way, though many from Pentecostal denominations believe that this "Baptism of the Holy Spirit" takes place after someone's salvation. This is a matter of interpretation; which hinges on how one understands the transition described in Acts 19:1-7—from John's baptism to Christ's baptism—and how the Holy Spirit is transitioning into the newness of the church, the body of Christ. It is a complicated concept to grasp at first, but as we mature in life, by living by faith, and studying the Scriptures, the Holy Spirit will help us fully understand how and when he works.

Who can perform baptisms? Scripturally, any Christian can baptize others, as Matthew 28 commands us, which is in line with the teaching of "the priesthood of all believers." This teaching is one of eight distinctive Baptist views and was held by the protestant reformer Martin Luther, and it is based mainly on First Peter 2:5-9 and Revelation 5:10, though other passages also support it.

If someone concludes that salvation is by grace alone and baptism has nothing to do with forgiveness or the washing away of sin, then the discussion of infant baptism is irrelevant. However, if someone believes that salvation comes through God's grace, plus man's efforts, then, infant baptism could be relevant. In the end, one's view of baptism is solely connected to their understanding of salvation as it relates to Christ's sacrifice and Man's nature.

Chapter 4

THE CANON AND ITS TRANSLATION

Within this chapter, we will be discussing the Protestant canon; how it has been translated into other languages; and how to choose the most reliable translations for reading and further study.

Jesus relied heavily on the Scriptures. Matthew 4:1-7 records how Satan placed three temptations before him, and how he responded each time with: "it is written..." In Matthew 21:42, he asked, "Did you never read in the Scriptures...?" placing an emphasis on their importance for answers from God. Mark 12:24 records Jesus responding to a question about morality; expecting those asking the questions to have found the answer in the Scriptures: "Jesus said to them, Is this not the reason you are mistaken, that you do not understand the Scriptures, or the power of God?"

We find in Luke 24:27, Jesus explains how the Scriptures spoke about him, and how he is the fulfillment of all they represent. "And beginning with Moses and with all the prophets, He explained to them the things concerning Himself in all the Scriptures." This concept is reaffirmed in John 5:39 when Jesus said, "You search the Scriptures, because you think that in them you have eternal life; and it is these that bear witness of Me ...." Jesus' statement reflects the fact that it is not the Scriptures that save us, but they do contain the written message of Jesus the Messiah, as their central theme. This is why he said in Matthew 5:17 "Do not think that I came to abolish the Law or the Prophets; I did not come to abolish, but to fulfil." On the night before he went to the cross to die, Jesus prayed to his heavenly Father: "Sanctify them in the truth; Thy word is truth." (John 17:17) This statement emphasizes that what God says is true and important, for God's words help set the standards for knowing how to be set apart from sin—which is what "sanctify" means—and they uncover Satan's methods for our physical and spiritual destruction.

"Until I come, give attention to the public reading of Scripture, to exhortation and teaching," was the urging of the Apostle Paul to his young protégé in First Timothy 4:13, to stress the importance of the Scriptures as God's truth to the early church.

Yes, the Scriptures are important, as they are the only historical record of what God has said and what he wants us to know. The reality is they are his direct revelation to humanity about knowing God's ethical and moral standards for distinguishing right from wrong in our everyday lives. Remember, morality is God's standard, not humankind's standard. Therefore, it is important that we understand the process that God used to bring us his wisdom, truth, and historical perspective.

TRANSLATION CONCEPTS

Because the Christian faith depends heavily on the Scriptures' authority, we need to understand why we can trust their truth and consistency. Back in the early 80s, there was a translation debate within the Christian community. Not a bad thing, but it did occasionally lead to some division and hard feelings. Today some churches will only use the King James Version of the Bible, referring to it as the "authorized version" or the only inspired Scripture in English for today's Christian. Is that a problem? My answer is no, as long as those with this view do not become critical, or judge fellow believers for not holding to the same view. It should be left up to the individual Christian to make that determination for themselves based on God's working in their lives.

This debate resulted in some good books that help us better understand how the Bible came to be. Two in particular are, *The King James Version Debate: A Plea for Realism* by D. A. Carson (still in print), and *The Translation Debate: What Makes a Bible Translation Good?* by Eugene H. Glassman. (Out of print) Both books have about 125 pages; they are very reliable and they have greatly helped me to understand what I am about to share with you.

TEXTUAL CRITICISM

THE NEW TESTAMENT

THE PROCESS

The vast majority of Christian theologians believe in the divine inspiration and inerrancy of the original Scriptures, even though we do not have those original documents. What we do have is about 5,000 partial manuscripts and about 50 copies of the complete Greek New Testament. So what process was used to discover what God truly said? Good question!

Textual critics are professional linguists and translators who examine all the manuscripts and historical data, comparing one copy against another to detect any errors in spelling, grammar, punctuation, or syntax. They do not interpret the text but evaluate the manuscripts in order to classify them as text-types. They also look for missing letters, words, sentences, or duplication of words or sentences, which occur in any copying process.

Errors in manuscripts have been categorized as unintentional—when a scribe miscopied or misheard what was being dictated—or intentional, when someone may have tried to correct what they thought were errors. However, if these corrections did not match other copies, the copyists would have just introduced errors of their own.

Remember, with no printing presses in those days, everything was copied and re-copied by hand.

Today we have copies from several parts of the world, dating from as early as the second century to beyond the twelfth century. Some were produced privately, though most of them are the work of professionals such as linguistically trained monks who dedicated their lives to copying. Their methods included single copies of one manuscript at a time; while multiple copies resulted from several monks writing down what a colleague dictated to them. This was the textual critic process, which created what I mentioned earlier as "text-types" or a final "critical text." Each manuscript was placed into one of four types, which were categorized according to the repetitive nature of the errors they contained. Any manuscript containing more than one style of error was considered mixed and categorized separately. There are four "text-types," but we will only examine the two that have proved to be the most reliable.

> **The Byzantine Text** — Of the manuscripts available to us, this group contains more than the other three text-types combined.[1] These manuscripts were mostly preserved in the Byzantine Empire and its associated communities; and several sources reveal that none of them are from earlier than the fourth century. The King James Version (KJV) of the Bible is based from this group through a very small sample collection of manuscripts, which came to be known as the "Textus Receptus" (TR).[2] The term "TR" came from the Latin thirteen years after the KJV was published and means: "the text you now have is received."
>
> **The Alexandrian Text** — These manuscripts, from Alexandria in Egypt, was prepared by trained scribes who desired to preserve the text, and they have excellent

credentials. This text-type came from manuscripts, which date from as early as the second century. Such an early dating would support claims that they are closest to the original documents. The translators of the New American Standard Version of the Bible (NASB) based their work on this group of manuscripts.

THE TRANSLATIONS DEVELOPED

Having dealt with textual errors and established a final text, we now run into a completely new set of issues: translating the final text into different languages for everyday people to read. By 1979, about seventeen hundred—or ninety-five percent—of the world's languages had complete or partial translations of some part of the Scriptures.[3]

The translation process involves two approaches: form-oriented and content-oriented. The form-oriented approach places emphasis on the original language to carry over its original meaning, word for word; but a different word-usage can make this process very difficult. The content-oriented method emphasizes the receptor language, or the language being translated into, and concentrates on transferring concept for concept. How does this work? The translator analyses the concepts to be conveyed from the original language and uses concepts that are culturally understood as an equivalent meaning in the receptor language. And because this translation process requires some interpretation, the risk and possibility of some error could occur. Many modern Bible translations are developed by groups of translators rather than by individuals to help prevent this possibility.

Having noted that the KJV comes from the Byzantine Text tradition, and the NASB from the Alexandrian Text tradition, it is worth knowing that the NIV comes from what scholars refer to as "eclectic" texts, which are the result of pulling translation information from multiple resources, with independent reviews of each source.

CHRISTIANITY 101

Rules Used in the Selection Process of the Canon

It is one thing to take manuscripts and sort out errors between them, but once the books are put together and we have what was said, what criteria were used to discern which books were God-inspired and which were not? The Old Testament was being used at the time of Christ, who referred to it in Luke 24:44 as the Law, the Prophets, and Psalms—, which is part of a wider segment, referred to as the Writings.

New Testament manuscripts—the gospels and the letters—came after Christ; and the discerning process became the responsibility of the Church. By the second century, as the Church spread, those in authority realized that they needed a process to prevent God's new revelation within these manuscripts from being lost. But what guidelines could they apply to decide what should be included in this new canon?

With so much teaching material on this subject from A to Z, I will seek to uncover the nature of the issues and explain the bottom-line truth about them from my research and perspective.

God through his infinite wisdom not only provided scriptural rules we currently use to interpret the Scriptures, but he also provided key statements within the Scriptures to help us to distinguish between what he has said and what someone else has said. Deuteronomy 18:20-22 states: "But the prophet who shall speak a word presumptuously in My name which I have not commanded him to speak, or which he shall speak in the name of other gods, that prophet shall die. And you may say in your heart, How shall we know the word which the Lord has not spoken? When a prophet speaks in the name of the Lord, if the thing does not come about or come true, that is the thing which the Lord has not spoken. The prophet has spoken it presumptuously; you shall not be afraid of him." Second Peter 3:14-16 similarly states: "Therefore, beloved, since you look for these things, be diligent to be found by Him in peace, spotless and blameless, and regard the patience of our Lord to be salvation; just as also our beloved brother Paul, according to the wisdom given him, wrote to you, as also in all his letters, speaking in them of these things, in which are some things hard to understand, which the untaught and unstable distort, as they do also the rest of the Scriptures, to their own destruction." Here is the earliest affirmation that Paul's letters should be considered as scriptural. As Peter affirms that Paul's writings should be included as part of the inspired collection of Scriptures; Paul provides a reminder in Second Timothy 3:16-17: "All Scripture is inspired by God and profitable for teaching, for reproof, for correction, for training in righteousness; that the man of God may be adequate, equipped for every good work." These verses collectively tell us that all Scriptures are God-inspired; not just the Old Testament, but now the emerging New Testament should be included as well. Second Peter 1:20-21 states: "But know this first of all, that no prophecy of Scripture is a matter of one's own interpretation, for no prophecy was ever made by an act of human will, but men moved by the Holy Spirit spoke from God."

The concept of the person of the Holy Spirit is clearly presented as a New Testament concept. By putting together the concepts that these verses develop, we can conclude that God does not lie; so everything he says is either true or will happen as he promises. We can also be sure that God has not only spoken in Old Testament times but has now revealed himself through his chosen men known as the Apostles.

The Church Fathers' criteria were that any Apostles' writings, which harmonize with the existing Scriptures—without any contradictions—must be considered as equally inspired by God. These writings had been highly circulated and widely accepted as authoritative words from God by the first-century church, so their canonical acceptance was almost a foregone conclusion.[4]

The Apostles wrote Twenty-three of the New Testament's twenty-seven books. A medical doctor who traveled extensively with the

Apostle Paul wrote the Gospel of Luke and the book of Acts. The books of James and Jude are believed to be written by Jesus' brother, who was a leader in the Christian church in Jerusalem. The book of Hebrews has an unnamed author, but many believe it to be written by the Apostle Paul.

The New Testament refers to four different individuals named James. James the brother of Jesus was determined to be the most likely author of the books called James and Jude, because the Apostle James died in 44 A.D., and these two books were determined to be written after his death.

Further study will show that other criteria were included within these canonical selections, but they are not as strong as the two we have examined. In any case, the second-century church had already accepted twenty-two books as belonging to the canon, which confirms the strength of these two criteria.

THE ISSUE OF PARAPHRASES

To paraphrase an idea or concept is to restate it in the same language, using simpler terms. For example, Romans 1:16 in the *New American Standard Bible* (NASB), states: "For I am not ashamed of the gospel, for it is the power of God for salvation to everyone who believes, to the Jew first and also to the Greek." *The Living Bible* (TLB,) a paraphrased version, restates it thus: "For I am not ashamed of this Good News about Christ. It is God's powerful method of bringing all who believe it to heaven. This message was preached first to the Jews alone, but now everyone is invited to come to God in this same way." I would view both versions as equally accurate and valuable.

However, in the NASB, Romans 1:1 states: "Paul, a bond servant of Christ Jesus, called as an apostle, set apart for the gospel of God...," while the paraphrased TLB reads: "Dear friends in Rome: This letter is from Paul, Jesus Christ's slave, chosen to be a missionary, and sent out to preach God's Good News." The paraphrase is an acceptable description for new Christians and for young children, whom it was meant to reach. However, for Christians who want to grow further in their understanding of the Scriptures, I would suggest this paraphrase misses an important point. An Apostle can be a sent missionary; but the more important issue was that Paul's authority as God's representative was being challenged by some in the early church, so Paul needed to assert his apostolic credential, rather than being seen as just another person (or missionary) sent to proclaim the good news.

Does this mean paraphrasing is a bad thing? In my reading on this issue, I discovered that for professional linguists and translators', paraphrasing is normal and even necessary within the translation process. The Living Bible, a paraphrase, is not a true translation because it has not come from a language other than English.

Get the point? In translation, one must try to convey an idea and its intended meaning into another language and culture, which may not have a word with the same meaning. For example, translating the English word "love" from the original language is extremely difficult, for the Greek language has four different words with four different meanings for "love." This indicates the difficulty of linguistic work and shows the need to understand the issues before passing judgment on any given translation. The key to evaluating English translations is to know your Bible and your theology, so you may evaluate the differences between translations in the same language and culture.

If any translation, as a whole, denies major historical doctrines of the faith—like the Jehovah Witnesses' *New World Translation*—then it should be ignored. But, evaluating differences is best achieved via an overall view of each book, rather than by side-by-side comparisons of each verse. For example, one KJV verse may clearly affirm Jesus' divinity. The same NASB reference may be less assertive, but it will carry other verses to support the case. This may be true in reverse, to show that good translations reflect a collective consensus, even if matching references do not match each other exactly. If you compare the KJV, the NASB, and the NIV with each other, you will find all three in very close agreement, which will help you to understand their differences and hence a better understanding of the truth. And is this not the goal of reading the Scriptures? Coming to an understanding of the truth and being obedient to it? As I stated in another book, "For biblical truth to be true, it must agree with all other biblical truth." [5]

THE OLD TESTAMENT

I am not going to say much about the Old Testament canon or how it was preserved, except that the textual critic process was the same as the New Testament. I understand that there are a couple of full copies of the Old Testament manuscripts, along with four primary sources used for translation: the Hebrew text; the Septuagint (LXX)—a Greek translation of the Old Testament, translated in the second and third century B.C.; the Masoretic text—developed around the ninth century using many other reliable sources; and the Dead Sea Scrolls which were discovered in caves in 1947 in Israel. Some of these Scrolls date back 1,000 years earlier than any previous manuscript, and it is interesting to note that the investigation of them has revealed few real differences from what we already had in the Old Testament.[6] This confirms to me that God's hand has clearly been in the preservation of his words, which should strengthen the belief of those within the Christian faith.

BIBLICAL HERMENEUTICS

Biblical Hermeneutics is the art and science of Scripture interpretation, and most Seminaries and some Christian Universities offer courses on this discipline. In the United States, hermeneutics is usually a single three-hour course, meeting for three hours a week over a sixteen-week period, referred to as semester hours. Some Schools may offer this as a five-hour course, meeting five hours a week over a ten-week period, and referred to as quarter hours. In either case, the curriculum may differ at any given institution because of the different approaches they may take. Therefore, we need to discuss these differences.

Textual criticism deals with copying errors in manuscripts and develops a critical text that represents the original as closely as possible. Hermeneutics provides us with the rules for correctly interpreting the text and the author's original intent. Homiletics is the art of preaching or interpreting biblical truths for everyday life application, with hermeneutics as the supporting foundation. Without a correct hermeneutical approach, one would end up misapplying the same Scriptures. It is my view that this hermeneutical issue is why there are many different groups within the Protestant movement.

The Roman Catholic Church approach to hermeneutics was greatly influenced by Thomas Aquinas, an Italian philosopher, and theologian, a great intellectual of his day who still has great influence in the field of philosophical thought.[7]

The Protestant movement takes multiple approaches. One is called the Grammatico-Historical Method, or literal approach, which teaches that the Scriptures often interpret themselves. Another approach focuses on allegorical interpretation, or spiritualizing the text; stressing that allegorical or spiritualizing the text is more frequent and thus the normal way to interpret the Scriptures. This method provides much more latitude in developing a doctrine that may be more acceptable, but may not reflect God's true intent based on the normal, customary usage of the original language. The Grammatico-Historical method recognizes there are allegorical passages, but believes that the Scriptures can be understood correctly through a more literal approach by using the normal and customary usage of words. In the end, the allegorical method leaves it up to the individual and translative traditions of groups to come up with a correct interpretation; rather than following set guidelines developed from the Scriptures for interpretation.

I personally use the Grammatico-Historical method; and recommend two books: *Biblical Hermeneutics* by Milton S. Terry (in print) and *The Interpretation of Prophesy* by Paul Lee Tan. (Currently out of print.) Both authors take the same approach to biblical hermeneutics but use different methods when they interpret prophecy. There is a third book called: *Protestant Biblical Interpretation* by Bernard Ramm and is still in print today.

There are other approaches, but I find that God wants us to know and understand his words, and he has provided built-in rules for a correct interpretation, therefore it is my view that the Grammatico-Historical Method should be the preferred method of every Christian.

The first hermeneutical rule is found in First Corinthians 2:12-14: "Now we have received, not the spirit of the world, but the Spirit who is from God, that we might know the things freely given to us by God, which things we also speak, not in words taught by human wisdom, but in those taught by the Spirit, combining spiritual thoughts with spiritual words. But a natural man does not accept the things of the Spirit of God; for they are foolishness to him, and he cannot understand them, because they are spiritually appraised."

What does this mean? It means that anyone who does not have the Holy Spirit living inside them by being born again—according to John 3:3-15—will not fully understand what God is trying to say within his Scriptures. True understanding only comes through the Holy Spirit's guidance. We know this to be true through Jesus' teachings, as expressed through the following Scriptures. "And the disciples came and said to Him, 'Why do You speak to them in parables?' And He answered and said to them, To you it has been granted to know the mysteries of the kingdom of heaven, but to them it has not been granted." (Matthew 13:10-11) Matthew 13:34-35 states, "All these things Jesus spoke to the multitudes in parables, and He did not speak to them without a parable, so that what was spoken through the prophet might be fulfilled, saying, 'I will open My mouth in parables; I will utter things hidden since the foundation of the world.'" We also read in Second Timothy 2:7, "Consider what I say, for the Lord will give you understanding in everything." And also in Luke 24:45-48: "Then He opened their minds to understand the Scriptures, and He said to them, Thus it is written, that the Christ should suffer and rise again from the dead the third day; and that repentance for forgiveness of sins should be proclaimed in His name to all the nations, beginning from Jerusalem. You are witnesses of these things." If understanding spiritual things came naturally, then why would God need to help us in the process? This is something to think about.

Another rule in hermeneutics is that in many cases the Scriptures are self-interpreting. Many times within Jesus' parables, he explains their meaning to the disciples, as well as making statements for the purpose of fulfilling the Old Testament Scriptures. You will find many New Testament Scriptures that explain or verify Old Testament Scriptures, so I will not try to list them all for you. With all this said, hermeneutics is an important part of Bible study, and I hope I have encouraged you to seek out additional information on your own.

As a reminder, I have provided this explanation because it is my view that this subject is the cause of the major differences between local churches today.

RECOMMENDED TRANSLATIONS

I recommend these translations for everyday use and study:

- The King James Version (KJV)
- The New King James Version (NKJV)
- The New American Standard Version of 1960—1977 (NASB)
- The Christian Standard Bible — 2017 (CSB)

Other translations I use for reference in study are:

- New International Version (NIV)
- American Standard Version of 1901 (ASV)
- Revised Standard Version (RSV)

Other Works

- The Living Bible (TLB) — This is a paraphrase edition of the Bible and not considered a formal translation. This work was done by Kenneth N. Taylor, a Christian author and founder of Tyndale House, a publishing company. This work was inspired by his desire to have a modern-day English Bible that everyone, particularly new Christians and children, could understand. Though it has sold over 40 million copies, I would not use this translation for serious study or for an in-depth understanding of the Christian faith. This version can be useful, as intended, for someone that has no experience with the Scriptures and is trying to understand its overall message.[8]

- The Updated New American Standard Version Bible (NASU)—I personally ignore this version because of what I see as its unacceptable changes from the original NASB.

Other English translations include the English Standard Version (ESV), the New Century Version (NCV), and the New Living Translation (NLT). But the list I recommend is what I use and trust for everyday study use. As you mature in your faith, and you feel more confident in evaluating translations, feel free to venture out and compare others for your consideration.

THE CANON AND ITS TRANSLATION

SOME COMMENTS

The point of biblical translations is not whether we have the exact words as spoken by God, but whether we have the exact concepts and thoughts, he wants us to know and understand. It is the view of professional translators, theologians, church leaders, and individual Christians that we do, and without any doctrinal error.

In the end, there are three positions taken by the vast majority of Western Protestant Christians around the world. (i) The first position relates to the recommended English translations just listed, representing God's revelation to us. They are divinely preserved and represent an error rate of zero: plenary—complete; inerrant—without errors; and verbal—coming to us in written form. (ii) The second position is that these translations are divinely preserved, plenary, and verbal; but they may contain some minor errors within an overwhelming consistency. (iii) The third position is held by a smaller group who believe that the 1611 A.D. King James Version is the only inspired Word of God we have in English. An even smaller minority may hold the extreme position: that the KJV is the only inspired Word of God we have in any language. As a word of caution, if you run into any group who hold this extreme view of the Scriptures, I recommend you follow Jesus' suggestion in Matthew 15:14—"Let them alone; they are blind guides of the blind. And if a blind man guides a blind man, both will fall into a pit."

In all my years of reading and studying the Word of God in English, I have found no contradictions concerning issues of doctrine, archaeology, science, culture, or prophecy. I will concede that within the 66 books, there may be a dozen or so passages that may be questioned for harmonic consistency, which is a question of interpretational opinion. However, I have never found any errors that would lead me to doubt that the Bible is anything but God's inspired

Word, and it can be trusted to provide us with information, guidance, and truth about the creator God and his plan for his creation.

As a side historical note: chapter separations—1,189 in all—were first printed with Wycliffe's English version in 1382; and verse designations came in the sixteenth century, with the Latin Vulgate edition published in 1555 and later with the English New Testament Geneva Bible published in 1560, [9] which was the English translation used before the KJV was translated in 1611 A.D. Few people today would be able to read an original printed copy of the KJV because of its *ſtrange ſpeling*, for a letter "s" looked like an "*ſ*," and *manye wordes* included an "e" that we no longer use. I have seen such a copy and tried to read it, knowing what it was supposed to have said, which only confirms my view that we need to have high-quality, accurate English translations for our times.

SUMMARY

Anyone who begins to read and learn this information for the first time may feel a little overwhelmed. This is why when studying any subject, it is better to take things one step at a time. When I was in college, majoring in Bible, I started out in a school that understood this view by designing its entire four-year program in a systematic manner, requiring one to take many classes in a particular sequence so to build one's knowledge through a system of progression. Even though I was a mature Christian at the time, I found this approach most helpful, and I am grateful for those who thought my training through.

I have tried a similar approach when laying out my books; and hopefully what I have presented makes some sense to you. From here, we will be moving on into the inside workings of the church, covering topics such as church polity, local church teachings, and how to choose a local church. So, come join me for Chapter 5.

THE CANON AND ITS TRANSLATION

CHAPTER ENDNOTES

1. D.A. Carson, *The King James Version Debate: A Plea for Realism* (Grand Rapids: Baker Book House, 1979), 26.

2. Carson, *The King James Version Debate*, 37.

3. Eugene H. Glassman, *The Translation Debate: What Makes a Bible Translation Good?* (Downers Grove: InterVarsity Press, 1981), 12.

4. http://www.gotquestions.org/canon-bible.html (Link note added for additional information for the reader.)

5. Ashbaucher, *Made in the Image of God*, 22.

6. http://www.allaboutarchaeology.org/dead-sea-scrolls.htm (Link note added for additional information for the reader.)

7. http://plato.stanford.edu/archives/sum2014/entries/aquinas/ (Link note added for additional information for the reader.)

8. http://www.bible-researcher.com/lbp.html (Link note added for additional information for the reader.)

9. Glassman, *The Translation Debate*, 37.

Chapter 5

HOW THE LOCAL CHURCH IS ORGANIZED

In this chapter I will cover how local churches function in their internal polity and biblical teaching and offer some suggestions on what to look for when choosing a local church to attend.

CHURCH POLITY

Church polity is a term used that covers the subject matter of the various forms of church government, as it relates to the organization and governance structures of locally autonomous, denominational, or hierarchical churches. These structures broadly cover statements of mission, faith, doctrine, and covers documents related to constitutions, tax structure, and incorporation; and include rules for governing officers, ministry offices, and membership.

These structures try to follow biblical guidelines, though different churches or denominations will be shaped by how they interpret these guidelines. Churches' more-essential structural elements are underpinned by legal requirements, while others may allow for more flexible Scriptural interpretation, perhaps desiring for consensus and harmony that prevents confusion or chaos from arising.

The Scriptures reflect this through the example of Moses. When leading over two million Israelites from Egypt to their new homeland proved to be so great, he followed Jethro's advice by appointing leaders to deal with the everyday issues that confronted them; for they were still in the wilderness and their survival depended on structure (Exodus

18:12-27). The church is no different today. Even though today's church government is more complex than the first-century church, the Scriptures clearly emphasize the requirements of order, wisdom, and understanding that guide our current church polity for today's culture.

The church has clear scriptural guidelines for church doctrine; leadership standards and selection; the giving of money to support ministries; a designated day of worship; for local church members to meet together regularly; and how to participate in the Lord's Supper and Baptism.

In a previous chapter, I listed several types of Protestant churches. These churches all have different systems of governance: from Episcopal, Presbyterian, Congregational to other churches more independently autonomous, structured under a combination of Pastor/Elder/Trustee models. The critical factors in all these systems are the scriptural interpretations they sought to implement or to restore at the time they began, and their efforts to pattern their leadership structure after the early church—according to how they interpreted the Scriptures. This is the key to the whole issue of the many denominations and types of churches. It all hinges on their interpretation of the Scriptures. However, it is important to remember that interpreting the scriptures is not the same as rewriting them to make them say what you want them to say!

Not everyone interprets the Scriptures in the same way, because of the issue of hermeneutics, an academic discipline we discussed in the last chapter. Having studied the "art and science of Scripture interpretation," it has made it easier for me to understand why some church leaders may be confused in the matter of scriptural interpretation. Not all leaders have been trained to the same degree in matters of biblical guidelines, linguistic rules, and cultural issues in biblical times.

Another consideration is how the Holy Spirit works in each individual's life, teaching progressively in stages—one lesson at a time.

HOW THE LOCAL CHURCH IS ORGANIZED

This means not everyone is on the same page for proper scriptural interpretation, and there is no real agreement to what the right page is.

Unfortunately, some leaders may be only nominally Christian, which will affect each church or denomination according to their place within the hierarchy. The same is true about the membership, for while there are many members who are Christians; some are not. Let me try to bring some clarity to these statements.

The universal church, or the "body of Christ," totally consists of Christians, who are the true source and remnant of the body of Christ. You become a member of this body at the moment of your salvation, not when you join a local church. In theory, every member of a local church should first be a Christian or part of the body of Christ, but in reality, many people join local churches who have never experienced salvation or being born-again, as expressed in John Chapter 3. They become members for many reasons: some join to be part of something good; or because their friends or relatives are members; and others because they want to do the right thing and serve God. Sadly, some join because they want to harm the church—because they serve another master.

How do we know these things to be true? Listen to what Jesus had to say about them: "Not everyone who says to Me, 'Lord, Lord,' will enter the kingdom of heaven; but he who does the will of My Father who is in heaven. Many will say to Me on that day, 'Lord, Lord, did we not prophesy in Your name, and in Your name cast out demons, and in Your name perform many miracles?' And then I will declare to them, 'I never knew you; depart from Me, you who practice lawlessness.'" (Matthew 7:21-23) The Apostle Paul also issued this warning: "Be on guard for yourselves and for all the flock, among which the Holy Spirit has made you overseers, to shepherd the church of God which He purchased with His own blood. I know that after my departure savage wolves will come in among you, not sparing the flock; and from among your own selves men will arise, speaking perverse things, to draw away the disciples after them." (Acts 20:28-30)

As I have stated, the Christian faith is spiritual warfare; and sadly, there are many spiritual and emotional casualties. You may hear there are hypocrites in the church; just as there are hypocrites in every walk of life; but I would not let that stop you from getting involved. This book's aim is to help you understand the inside workings of the church; so you will simultaneously be prepared for the battles that will come and understand the many issues of our faith. As a result, you will be more stable as a Christian, as well as a stabilizing influence within the local church. For even in the midst of the warfare, we may experience the Holy Spirit's joy, peace, and understanding as he unifies us with God. Remember this encouragement from the Apostle Paul: "And the peace of God, which surpasses all comprehension, shall guard your hearts and your minds in Christ Jesus." (Philippians 4:7)

Spiritual warfare is behind many of the divisive issues among the local churches and is why some see differing forms of hypocrisy. The Christian faith is a spiritual battle, and Satan; the enemy of God and his universal church; is working overtime to deceive and to turn humanity away from God's Kingdom. This is why we are warned: "Be of sober spirit, be on the alert. Your adversary, the devil, prowls about like a roaring lion, seeking someone to devour. But resist him, firm in your faith, knowing that the same experiences of suffering are being accomplished by your brethren who are in the world." (1 Peter 5:8-9) And why Christ prophesied over the Apostle Peter: "And I also say to you that you are Peter, and upon this rock I will build My church; and the gates of Hades shall not overpower it." (Matthew 16:18)

Christ is the chief cornerstone—or foundation—of the church, so Satan's limited power will never shake this foundation. For the universal church—the body of Christ—is moving forward in spreading the Kingdom message of the Gospel. The more we understand the issues, the better prepared we will be to overcome these obstacles with the help of the Holy Spirit, so no one becomes listed among the spiritual casualties.

ISSUES OF INCORPORATION

Churches incorporate for two reasons. Firstly, to gain official recognition for practical matters, such as world mission support issues related to ordination; and secondly for legal liabilities, taxation, and other legal issues a church may face within meeting governmental business law requirements. These reasons can either simplify or complicate how churches implement their wider biblical mandates.

Under corporate law, a constitution or bylaws are required of churches, and these encompass the issue of local church membership. Is local church membership commanded by Scripture or is it strictly a legal issue tied to incorporating bylaws? This is a matter of interpretation of the Scriptures, which could be argued both ways. One would think that this issue of membership is not a matter of heaven or hell, and it should not be; but if any local church or denomination requires all new members to be baptized according to their traditions, new issues of interpretation arise. It is my view that church membership and baptism should be treated as two different events, but in reality, this is not always the case.

ISSUES OF MEMBERSHIP

My position on this issue is not just a matter of Scripture interpretation, but also a matter of common sense. The Holy Spirit placed the Apostle Philip on the same road as the Ethiopian eunuch where Philip showed him how to understand the Gospel. When the eunuch made a commitment to follow Christ, he wanted to be baptized right away, and he was. He then traveled back home. My question is, What local church did he just join? The answer: none! He became a Christian and part of "the body of Christ," a member of the universal

Church; he was then baptized by immersion to display his willingness to be identified with Christ in front of all his servants that were with him. Then, when they came out of the water, the Holy Spirit snatched Philip away and the eunuch was standing there alone. Philip didn't even get to stay long enough to discuss church membership! (Acts 8:26-40) It could be that when the eunuch got home, he started his own local church—something to think about!

I am not trying to arm anyone with arguments over membership polity with any local church, but simply to help you understand the issues. Then you will not be confused when you read the Scriptures and then deal with local church polity. If you were baptized by immersion, and a local church asks you to be re-baptized to meet their membership rules, feel free to do so. Your obedience was recognized in the sight of God the first time around, so if you have to jump through any hoops to belong to a local church, the decision is up to you.

Most local churches tie baptism to membership, to bring simplicity to a complicated system. When anyone is converted through the Holy Spirit, that person becomes a member of the universal Church. But not all individuals at conversion are baptized in obedience to Christ. From the time of conversion, the Holy Spirit begins to lead a person to where they will grow spiritually, which is usually a local Christian church.

The local church has been mandated with authority and with the responsibility to disciple new Christians to maturity. This mandate requires protecting the integrity of that local church's doctrine and leadership, so nonbelievers may be kept out of its governance while developing a system of membership that reveals the reality of people's conversion and their intent to maintain regular attendance. Baptism is sometimes required within the entry to membership, as a public testimony of your identity and your spiritual commitment to Christ. Often this is not an issue, because there are many new Christians who have never been baptized and who should be—as Jesus commanded (Matthew 28).

HOW THE LOCAL CHURCH IS ORGANIZED

So, do the Scriptures teach that baptism is synonymous with joining a local church? It is my view that it does not. Consider today's world culture. Becoming a local church member may mean your name is associated with a denomination that may be targeted for criticism or even persecution by some governments. Just being baptized does not require your name to be identified with any organization, thus escaping possible persecution. I recall one foreign couple who regularly attended a local church in the United States but did not become members, lest their family be targeted by the hostile government in their home country. The real issue here was not membership, but the fact the local church would not baptize them because they did not want to become members.

This is one of several reasons why I believe membership and baptism should be considered separately. Some churches will allow non-members limited participation, while others will not allow any participation without membership. Membership has its legitimate purposes, but it sometimes can become an issue when not approached biblically. Church attendance does not constitute church participation or require church membership, so if you just want to attend a church and not get any more involved, then our discussion about membership is a moot point.

If you decide to become a member of a church, you are agreeing to what is written within its bylaws; doctrinal statements; statements of faith; leadership criteria; organization's voting rights, and the church's corporate or private disciplinary processes. This is not only a spiritual issue but also a legal one; as with any organization like Boy Scouts, YMCA, PGA, and Unions. This system has served the church well for hundreds of years, though sometimes-cultural considerations have brought changes to membership rules. Unfortunately, some churches have allowed cultural considerations to dictate some doctrinal changes when they should not have. How the church organizes itself is one thing, but the scriptural truths, which the church should be supporting and defending, should never be changed. Malachi 3:6 declares that God does not change; and Matthew 24:35 declares God's word is forever: "Heaven and earth will pass away, but My words shall not pass away."

Concluding my comments on the issue of membership, I would like to speak to the issue of monetary support for God's work through the local church. All churches teach their own perspective on the subject of giving, so I will limit my comments as follows: The support of God's work is not an issue of local membership, but an issue of obedience of all those that are members of the universal church worldwide. I support my comments based on the following Scriptural examples and if further studied would be supported by a wider perspective expressed throughout all the Scriptures.

Within the Old Testament, we find the example of Abram, who made an offering to God's High Priest Melchizedek, as found in Genesis 14:18-20. This display of giving was an act to honor and show appreciation towards God, the provider of all that we have. This act had no connection to the Mosaic Law; because the incident took place about 500 years before the Law was written. Within the New Testament, we are given examples of giving of time and monetary funds in support of God's work, as found in Romans 15:15-19, Ephesians 5:1-2 and Second Corinthians 9:6-9. There are other Scriptures that could be discussed on this topic, but the only point I want to make here is simply this: the status of one's membership to any local church does not negate the Christian's responsibility to honor God through giving of time or monetary funds.

This is a principle that, if honored with a correct attitude, God's blessings are not unnoticed.

LOCAL CHURCH TEACHINGS

Every local church should be teaching the foundational truths or doctrines which we covered in Chapter 3. The Scriptures contain hundreds of principles that deal with everyday issues in life, such as handling money, close relationships, wider relationships, morality, and ethics, to mention a few. There is always some room for the interpretation of these, which is why churches offer different teaching on them. Some churches offer no teaching at all, while others go all-out and try to teach everything they can about how the Scriptures relate to everyday life.

It is always wise to measure whatever is being presented to you, against the widest scriptural context. What do I mean by that? I mean, one should never build a (foundational) belief, which is supported by only a single verse. Good teaching gains its authority from having consistent and repeated support from multiple scriptural sources, and it builds a firm base for our unity and our confidence in Christ. However, the final approval should come from the Holy Spirit within you, as he confirms the truth of what is being said or taught. John's gospel describes him as the Spirit of truth, for the Holy Spirit will never lead you to any conclusion that contradicts the concepts and principles within the Scriptures. Remember, there are no contradictions in Scripture; for biblical truth to be true, it must agree with all other biblical truth. For confirmation, read what John Chapters 14 through 17 say about the Holy Spirit and about what truth is; and then you can compare these concepts with what the rest of the Scriptures reveal.

THE ISSUE OF SCRIPTURAL PHILOSOPHY

Scriptural Philosophy is how I describe one's systematic approach to one's biblical theology in order to teach others, which I will try to explain as clearly as possible.

Theological training includes various approaches to studying and understanding the Scriptures. The major ones are Systematic Theology, Biblical Theology, Dogmatic Theology, and Philosophical Theology. These approaches all include five major concepts regarding the primary message of the Gospel, and of God's working in the world. The first two concepts deal more with how God's covenants are viewed and how prophesies are seen and interpreted. The third and fourth concepts deal with God's sovereignty throughout the Scriptures with a relationship to humanity and the salvation process. The fifth view deals with how one views God's commandments and standards for everyday living. These five "Scriptural Philosophies" are called Covenant or Reformed theology, Dispensational theology, Calvinism, Arminianism, and Legalism; and they cause the biggest debates within the Christian community.

Covenant Theology

Covenant Theology became a developing system in the seventeenth century and is associated with the Presbyterians and the Westminster Confession of Faith, with another form associated with "Baptist Covenant Theology" or "1689 Federalism," and was not a direct product of the Protestant Reformation movement. It sees the Old Testament and all its covenants as one system of works and sees the New Testament as a system of grace alone. This approach holds that the New Covenant replaces the Old Covenant, but it includes all Old Testament covenants. Many church leaders and prominent Christian writers and theologians have espoused and promoted this theological system, which sounds very logical and convincing on the surface.

How does this affect one's foundational understanding of the Christian faith? It doesn't, but it does help you to understand the role of Israel within the Scriptures and the world we live in today, as well as providing an understanding of God and Man's part in the salvation process. It will also influence your studies in the area of eschatology, which is the study of "last things" or "end times" as laid out in Scripture.

This view offers its followers a total view of the Scriptures, but if you do not hold to this scriptural philosophy, it will not keep you out of heaven or put you in wrong standing with God. It is merely a philosophy of interpretation that will help you have a better understanding of certain Scriptural teachings.

Dispensational Theology

Dispensational theology recognizes the same covenants that covenant theologians do, but sees these covenants as working separately towards the single goal of humanity's final judgment, which includes salvation for those who put their faith in Christ alone. Dispensational theologians interpret the Abrahamic Covenant as the foundation for the Mosaic, Davidic, and New Covenants, which each reflect different stages of God's working throughout history. They identify these stages as showing how God is working differently in a progression towards achieving his plan for the world. These stages—as the Scriptures reveal—are the time of the Old Testament; the time of the Gentiles—or the "church age;" and the time to come, which Christ called the end of the age. (See Matthew Chapter 24)

Classical Dispensationalists have expanded these three into seven distinct dispensations of time, mostly from the Old Testament. Their scriptural bases come from Ephesians 1:8-10; 3:2-9; Colossians 1:25-27; Acts 1:6-8; 17:30; Luke 21:24; and 2 Corinthians 3:7-9. If you compare these verses in the KJV, NASB, ASV of 1901, and the RSV, you will find many of them using the terms "dispensation" or "administration," providing context to what a dispensation is—an administration of time—the method God was administering his dealings with humanity.

Covenant theologians will claim John Darby of the eighteenth century as the father of this system, but early Church apologist Justin Martyr (100—168 A.D.) recognized the premillennial position of dispensational theology; making reference to the writings of the Apostle John,[1] as did the early church for the first 300 years from its inception. This view was set aside when Origen's (185—250 A.D.) allegorical interpretation created a position of Amillennialism, which Augustine (354—430 A.D.) also supported. There was no re-emphasis on this issue until the Protestant Reformation restored the hermeneutical approach of literal interpretation. Later, through John Darby's literal hermeneutical approach, dispensational theology was reintroduced to the church. Since then, dispensational theology has been developing into a variety of perspectives; which has resulted in some confusion.

My studies in Premillennialism have given me a desire to write a systematic explanation on this subject, in hopes to dispel growing misnomers and help those interested in this view come to a better understanding to its true dynamics. In June 2019 I completed a textbook on this subject called *Dispensational Theology: A Textbook on Eschatology in the Twenty-First Century*, which should provide you with some foundation to understanding the concepts involved.

Calvinism

Calvinism is a theological view named after John Calvin (1509—1564 A.D.), a French lawyer who turned pastor and theologian; and a statesman who never held public office. John Calvin proceeded Martin Luther and continued to develop the Reformation. Though Calvin and Luther shared similar theological viewpoints, their personalities were total opposites.

Calvinism stresses that people have no free will to be saved or lost; so human salvation is strictly God's choice. Calvin's teaching on Salvation can be summarized through the following acronym, **TULIP**:

- Total Depravity of Man: Man's nature is totally depraved and he cannot seek God on his own.

- Unconditional Election: God elects or chooses who will and will not be saved. It is totally God's choice and humankind has no choice in the matter.

- Limited Atonement: Christ only died for the elect, or God's chosen. Jesus did not die for the world, but only for those, he has chosen to be saved from their sins.

- Irresistible Grace: God's call to be saved, cannot be resisted by humankind.

- Perseverance of the Saints: The salvation of humankind can never be reversed. It is permanent!

Calvin's prominent influence within Protestantism and his approaches to Scripture have contributed to differences within various churches and denominations today.

Arminianism

Arminianism is the result of the teaching of Jacobus Arminius (1560—1609 A.D.), a Dutch Reformed theologian, and who proceeded John Calvin. The original Armenian position is best expressed in the Five Articles of Remonstrance as summarized here:

- Salvation is by God's enabled faith.

- The Atonement; or Christ's death is adequate for all.

- Salvation comes through the work of the Holy Spirit. Humankind does not have the ability to have faith in his own will power.

- Believers' ability to do "good" is only accomplished through the power of the Holy Spirit, though humankind does have the ability to resist the Holy Spirit's working in one's life.

- Believers have full power to resist sin through the grace of God, but the believer's ability to reject God's grace is still an unknown question that needs further review.

The long version of these articles can be found on the Internet. They are very educational but not entirely reflective of how some Calvinists present Arminianism.

Legalism

Legalism is a philosophy of misunderstanding. The best way to understand this is through Matthew 15:1-9, which records Jesus' conversation with Jewish religious rulers called Pharisees.

> Then some Pharisees and teachers of the law came to Jesus from Jerusalem and asked, 'Why do your disciples break the tradition of the elders? They don't wash their hands before they eat!' Jesus replied, 'And why do you break the command of God for the sake of your tradition? For God said, 'Honor your father and mother' and 'Anyone who curses his father or mother must be put to death.' But you say that if a man says to his father or mother, 'Whatever help you might otherwise have received from me is a gift devoted to God, he is not to honor his father with it.' Thus you nullify

the word of God for the sake of your tradition. You hypocrites! Isaiah was right when he prophesied about you: "These people honor me with their lips, but their hearts are far from me. They worship me in vain; their teachings are but rules taught by men." (NIV)

Jesus' comments show that these religious rulers and teachers had over time replaced the true interpretation of the Scriptures with their own traditions. This is the true meaning of legalism; by which some within the church have also—over time—tried to replace what the Scriptures, as a whole, teach regarding God's intent and heart with their own unbalanced perspectives; and then tried to impose those views as a standard for all other believers to follow. We must be on guard against this activity within any local church or denomination, as it, unfortunately, happens often.

To understand how Legalism misunderstands what the Scriptures teach as a whole, let us look at some examples. God commands us to be holy for he is holy by nature (Leviticus 11:45, 1 Peter 1:16). This truth is clearly declared by God in both the Old and New Testaments. And how do we become holy? God makes us holy only through the death of Jesus Christ on the cross of Calvary. Christians do not usually misunderstand this. Nevertheless, while we live on this earth, our experience of holiness is to be increasingly separated from sin, as we grow in the knowledge and wisdom of the Lord. This separation is called progressive sanctification, and it is within this sanctification process that legalism begins to creep in. Jesus said: "If you love me, you will keep my commandments" (John 14:15), and "A new commandment I give to you, that you love one another, even as I have loved you, that you also love one another. By this all men will know that you are My disciples, if you have love for one another." (John 13:34-35)

Legalists take the do's and don'ts of the Scriptures and twist them to mean something different. Or it adds to them with expectations for every Christian to follow—regardless of their spiritual maturity or their personal journey with God—demanding perfect obedience to what they see as the letter of the law; and forgetting the spirit of the law or the very heart of God. All because they fail to understand how the New Covenant works. God states he will put his laws in the believer's heart to teach them his ways, not by keeping the letter of the law but by surrendering to the will of God who indwells them. It is only his inner presence that gives them a new attitude and power to be obedient to what the Scriptures teach. **ATTITUDE** is the key.

In reviewing these scriptural philosophies, we should realize that most Christians do not hold to any single version, but come to a blending of them through studying the Scriptures. Many Christians select points from both Calvinism and Arminianism to come to what they see as a more balanced perspective; but how you decide your view will be between you and the Holy Spirit, your ultimate teacher.

The blending of Covenant Theology and Dispensational Theology would be more difficult because these views are based on two opposite premises.

It should also be noted that many who hold to the five points of Calvinism also hold to Covenant or Reformed theology, although some prominent church leaders are Calvinistic in their theology and hold to a dispensational view of eschatology. Again, what you decide about what you believe about these issues will be determined on your hermeneutical approach and the work of the Holy Spirit in your life.

Someone recently asked me if the Holy Spirit teaches everyone a different truth. That is a good question; and my answer was that every Christian is on a different knowledge level or understanding of biblical truth; because understanding is partly based on knowledge, and our development of biblical truth comes to us in stages. Today I understand something one way, but gaining new information may enhance my understanding. This is how the Holy Spirit works in our lives; teaching us according to what we know and helping us at different points in our understanding. In most cases, it is the same truth, but our conclusions may differ based on our current knowledge. However, if we were given enough time in life, the Holy Spirit would bring everyone to the same conclusion on any biblical truth.

Some may consider my view on this as erroneous thinking, but from my understanding of the Scriptures as a whole, I will stand on this summary. The Apostle Paul expresses it this way: "For we know in part, and we prophesy in part; but when the perfect comes, the partial will be done away. When I was a child, I used to speak as a child, think as a child, reason as a child; when I became a man, I did away with childish things. For now we see in a mirror dimly, but then face to face; now I know in part, but then I shall know fully just as I also have been fully known." (1 Corinthians 13:9-12)

CHRISTIAN FUNDAMENTALISM

Before we move on, let us clarify the meaning of Fundamentalist or Fundamentalism. These terms are misunderstood by many throughout the world, through being demonized over the years for various reasons.

Christian Fundamentalism represents a biblical view that was developed in the 19th century to combat the liberal theology that was creeping up in the church. It states that there are fundamental doctrines or teachings essential to the Christian faith; and today it is primarily associated with some Non-denominational, Evangelical, and Baptist churches. It began with five fundamental doctrines, but some proponents have added up to five additional doctrines. The original five doctrines are as follows:

1. The inerrancy of Scripture

2. The virgin birth of Christ
3. The death, burial, and resurrection of Christ
4. The atoning work of Christ
5. The visible and physical second coming of Jesus Christ

The foundational doctrines of all churches would align with these teachings, but liberal theology began to deny/question some of these fundamental truths. Some felt it necessary to emphasize this list, to remind their members of what the Scriptures teach. Any Christian who says they are a fundamentalist is saying that they believe in these fundamental teachings of the Christian faith. There are those that have added to this list, which has caused some issues within the Fundamentalist Movement, because not everyone using this term may agree with the additions. For further discussion on the issue of fundamentalism vs. liberalism, you can visit http://www.theopedia.com/The_Fundamentals or pick up R. A. Torrey's book, *The Fundamentals: A Testimony to the Truth*.

THINGS TO CONSIDER IN CHOOSING A LOCAL CHURCH

When you consider joining and becoming part of a local church, I recommend you ask yourself these questions:

1. Is the Bible used, in every pulpit sermon, as the authority backing the message?

2. Does the church put emphasis on missionary work—locally and around the world?

3. Does the church have an educational program for the family? It could be in any of these forms: Sunday School, Adult Bible

Studies, Home Bible Studies, Youth Ministries, Children Ministries, Singles Ministries, Discipleship Ministries, or Catechisms. Though this would depend on the size of the church, all local churches should have some form of education or disciple ministry for the edification of believers.

4. What does this church believe and teach concerning the major doctrines of the Bible? If you do not know what these doctrines are, I recommend a review of Chapter 3. Most churches will have a church constitution and a statement of faith for you to read, but if any church does not make any such documents available for you to review, then I would recommend looking for another church unless of course, this church is part of the persecuted church that has moved underground to protect itself.

5. Does the church hold its leadership to be spiritually and legally accountable? This is usually included within its governance; which may vary between Congregational, Presbyterian or Episcopal rule, and many independent churches, function with some form of Pastoral/Deacon/ Trustee governance.

6. What outward signs reflect a church having problems?

- Lack of love for one another, which may take a little time and some involvement on your part to detect. Jesus said; you will know they are my disciples if they have a love for one another. (John 13:35)

- An overemphasis on giving money. The Scripture speaks of money more than any other subject. However, when sermons or in-house discussions regularly overemphasize the subject of giving money, this may be a sign of spiritual problems within that local body, since giving is a matter of the heart and the leading of the Holy Spirit. Whether the problem is with the congregation or with leadership or both, there is a problem that needs to be addressed.

- Does the only authority on spiritual matters come from the historical doctrinal teachings of the Bible, or does it come from one person's private interpretation? If it is the second, it could be a religious cult, which Walter Martin's book *The Kingdom of the Cults* (First Edition) defines as a group of people gathered about a specific person or person's private interpretation of the Bible. Religious cults include groups like the Mormons—who follow the teachings of Joseph Smith and Brigham Young; Jehovah Witnesses—who follow the teachings of Charles T. Russell and J. F. Rutherford; Christian Science—which follows the teachings of Mary Baker Eddy; and the Unity School of Christianity—who follow the teachings of Charles and Myrtle Filmore.

When looking for a local church, make sure that you look for one that teaches the historic doctrines of the Christian faith, rather than one that has embraced major doctrinal changes that have come after the sixteenth century. In the end, you need to remember the church is the single body of Christ, worldwide, and this body gathers locally in the form of New Testament local church.

7. How do I know what church God wants me to attend?

- The Holy Spirit is your teacher and guide. Pray and listen to Him. (John 14:26)

- Make a checklist of some things mentioned here. If the church is practicing things that are unbiblical in a big way, look somewhere else. Example: The ordination of homosexuals, immoral lifestyles of leadership and membership with no accountability, the denial that Jesus Christ is God incarnate, the downplaying of the importance of the "Word of God" (the Bible) in the Christian's life and false teachings of other major doctrines.

- Does this church fit the spiritual needs I have in my life or in my family's life?

- Is there something I can contribute, through my God-given spiritual gifts, to this local body for the work of the ministry and the edification of other believers? (1 Corinthians 12:1-31)

Remember, there is no perfect local church, we are all sinners saved by grace and the Bible teaches that God's Kingdom is being advanced by the Holy Spirit, as he works through the efforts of local New Testament churches.

PRAYER

If you have never prayed before, or if you would like to know more about prayer as it relates to the Christian faith, then the following comments hopefully will help provide some direction in this area. Prayer is simply talking to God using your own words. Jesus gave us an example of how to pray in Matthew 6:9-13:

After this manner therefore pray ye: Our Father which art in heaven, Hallowed be thy name. Thy kingdom come. Thy will be done in earth, as it is in heaven. Give us this day our daily bread. And forgive us our debts, as we forgive our debtors. And lead us not into temptation, but deliver us from evil: For thine is the kingdom, and the power, and the glory, for ever. Amen. (KJV)

What is Jesus telling us here? Simply this! **Our Father which art in heaven**: recognizes that God is in heaven as a superior being to humankind. **Hallowed be thy name**: Is recognition of God's Holiness. **Thy kingdom come**: Prioritizes God's kingdom above our desires. **Thy will be done in earth, as it is in heaven:** Teaches us to seek God's will for our lives as he has sovereignly planned. **Give us this day our daily bread:** God provides us with what we need on a daily basis and this urges us not to be presumptuous or to ask for more than we need from day today. **And forgive us our debts, as we forgive our debtors:** Reflecting that we should ask God to forgive our sins against him daily, as we in like manner should forgive others who sinned against us daily. **And lead us not into temptation, but deliver us from evil:** This statement is asking God to alert us to the temptation of sin and to provide us a path away from evil in all its forms. **For thine is the kingdom, and the power, and glory, for ever:** This is a recognition that in the end, God is holy and worthy to be praised in honor and glory. **Amen:** A word reflecting agreement with this prayer.

This prayer reflects the elements that make up a good conversation when talking or praying to God. Do I have to include all these elements in all my prayers? No, not necessarily. This prayer simply reflects what our attitude should be when we speak to our heavenly Father; and things we should be practicing in our daily lives.

HOW THE LOCAL CHURCH IS ORGANIZED

As you read the Scriptures, you will find there are things we are instructed to do, like, be thankful, be joyful, be forgiving, show love for each other. So in prayer, we can incorporate these things. How would that look in our prayers? We can start out by recognizing and praising who God is, moving into thanking him for who he is: holy, merciful, all-powerful, loving, and—a very important attribute—never changing. Why is that important? Because if God's nature could ever change, we could never be sure of his perspective or how consistent his actions would be, and he would then become an unstable force in our world. This would be a fearful thing, as God himself in Malachi 3:6 states: "For I, the Lord, do not change; therefore you, O Sons of Jacob, are not consumed." From this part of one's prayer, you can ask God to forgive your shortcomings for the day and pray for your own needs and for the needs of others. Pray for yourself and your family's protection from evil and evil-doers. In the end, prayer is simply, in your own words, praising God and asking Him for guidance and help.

We are told in other parts of Scripture that when we pray, we should pray with a correct attitude and not with selfish motives (James 4:3), such as God give me this or that because I need it for selfish purposes.

There is a great deal that could be said about prayer, and there are many books on the subject. I have merely presented a quick guide to get you started on a correct approach to prayer and to encourage you to seek out other books dedicated to the subject to learn more.

A frequently asked question about prayer is; Why do we pray? The really short answer is because it humbles us before God and draws us closer to Him in our personal relationship. Think of it this way, if you fell in love with someone, made a lifelong commitment, and married him or her. Would it then make sense to ignore them and never hold any conversation? Prayer is holding a conversation with God as your heavenly Father, and with Jesus Christ who scriptures depict as the bridegroom, with us as his bride, this makes us spiritually married to God—something to think about!

SUMMARY

If you are a new Christian or one who has never been exposed to these issues or facts, it has been my hope you have not been too confused by what has been expressed here. My intention has been to provide you with what I felt, was important and relevant to your spiritual journey and research of the Christian faith.

If you are not a Christian and you are reading this material, it is my hope that you find what you are looking for here. But in the end, whatever your status in life, here you have a snapshot of Christianity 101, representing the foundational truths of the Christian faith.

Within our next chapter, you will find an essay on the book of Romans; which I felt was a good chapter to end on. Understanding the book of Romans is key to understanding this book's content, so I hope you will spend the time evaluating it.

I have not spoken on how to apply the Scriptures to everyday life, so I will make the following recommendations of good literature by trusted Christian authors. As life's questions come and you begin to seek for answers and the desire to understand the Christian faith further, these ministering authors listed below can be found on the Internet or in many cases in your Christian bookstores. Feel free to use these resources as supplemental help to your daily Bible reading or study.

- Warren W. Wiersbe—Pastor, Bible Teacher and Author of more than 150 books.

- Chuck Swindoll—Pastor, Radio Bible Teacher, and Author of over 70 books.

- John MacArthur—Pastor, Radio Bible Teacher, and Author of over 250 books.

- David Jeremiah—Pastor, Radio Bible Teacher, and Author of several books.

- Jay Ashbaucher—Retired Pastor, Bible Teacher, and Author of several books.

CHRISTIANITY 101

Chapter Endnotes

1. http://www.ldolphin.org/premillhist.html (Link note added for additional information for the reader.)

Chapter 6

THE BOOK OF ROMANS: AN ESSAY PERSPECTIVE ON ITS TEACHINGS ABOUT THE CHURCH

To understand the book of Romans will require some knowledge of its author and of its secular and religious historical settings. Then we can begin to recognize the need for such a book and thus its theology, which we will divide into sections that will build on each other to bring us to a final conclusion.

THE HISTORY

God used Alexander the Great and his Greek vision for the world in 333 to 323 B.C., to shape New Testament times.[1] By the first century, Rome had established two hundred years of overall political stability, using Greek culture to shape its Empire.[2] What was the society like in the days of Christ? Eduard Lohse makes this observation:

"Superstition and notions of fate, the yearning for miracles and fascination with astrology and magic, all of which found numerous adherents in the Hellenistic period, make it evident that people were in the throes of deep anxiety and uncertainty about life. Threatened by powers and demons, by illnesses and unforeseen strokes of fate, one lived in suspense and fear and felt subject to overpowering forces against which one could not assert oneself." [3]

A contemporary cultural influence resulted from the Jewish wars, starting with the Maccabean revolt in 169 B.C. By 165 B.C., a treaty allowed for self-governance in many matters including freedom of religion, but it stopped short of true political freedom.[4] The Pharisees' sect emerged as a result, and spread via the network of synagogues throughout the Diaspora. Their teachings focused mainly on keeping the law, the Sabbath, purification rights,[5] and raising the oral traditions of past generations to equality with the Law of Moses. These traditions were later recorded in the Mishnah and Talmud.[6] Fausset's Bible Dictionary makes the following observations:

> The Mishnah or "second law," the first portion of the Talmud, is a digest of Jewish traditions and ritual, put in writing by rabbi Jehudah the Holy in the second century BC. The Gemara is a twofold "supplement," or commentary: firstly of Jerusalem until the first half of the fourth century; and secondly that of Babylon B.C. 500. The Mishnah has six divisions (on seeds, feasts, women's marriage, etc., decreases and compacts, holy things, clean and unclean), and an introduction on blessings. Hillel and Shammai were leaders of two schools of the Pharisees, differing on slight points; the Mishnah refers to both (living before Christ) and to Hillel's grandson, who was Gamaliel, Paul's teacher. In an ironic twist, the gospels identify most of Jesus' opponents as Pharisees; but throughout Acts, the Sadducees were more opposed to the church than the Pharisees. Because the Pharisees believed in resurrection; which was one of the key teachings of the church, (Mark 9:10; Acts 1:22; 2:32; 4:10; 5:31; 10:40) regarded Christians as their allies against the Sadducees (John 11:57; 18:3; Acts 4:1; 5:17. In Acts 23:6-9, Paul raised this common belief when he was brought before the Sanhedrin—the Jewish Council. The Mishnah lays down the fundamental principle of the Pharisees. "Moses received the oral law from Sinai, and delivered it to Joshua, and Joshua to the elders, and these to the prophets, and these to the men

of the great synagogue" (Pirke Aboth, 1). The absence of directions for prayer, and of mention of a future life, in the Pentateuch probably gave a pretext for the figment of a traditional oral law.[7]

Another influential figure during Paul's first three missionary journeys was Emperor Claudius, who ruled from 41 to 54 A.D. In his awareness of religious issues, he recognized the tension between Jews and Christians and—according to the biographer Suetonius—expelled the Jews from Rome for a short time during the period of troubles. Christians may have been expelled as well, for Acts 18:2 makes mention of how Paul met Aquila and Priscilla in Corinth.

More widely, Claudius supported the Jews as a people and confirmed their existing rights and privileges. In Alexandria he once tried to protect the Jews without provoking Egyptian nationalism, for in a surviving letter addressed to the city of Alexandria, he asked Jews and non-Jews "to stop this destructive and obstinate mutual enmity." Although personally disinclined to accept divine honors, he did not seriously oppose that trend and had a temple erected to himself in Camulodunum,[8] which is currently the city of Colchester in Essex. All this plays a role in our attempt to understand the "why" or purpose and theology of the book of Romans.

THE AUTHOR

Fausset's Bible Dictionary has the following introduction to the Apostle Paul:

> Though of purest Hebrew blood (Phil. 3:5), 'circumcised the eighth day, of the stock of Israel, of the tribe of Benjamin, (bearing the name of the eminent man of that tribe, King Saul,) a Hebrew of the Hebrews,' yet his birthplace was the Gentile Tarsus. (Acts 21:39, "I am a Jew of Tarsus in Cilicia,

a citizen of no mean city.") His father, as himself, was a Pharisee (Acts 23:6). Tarsus was celebrated as a school of Greek literature (Strabo, Geogr. 1:14). Here he acquired that knowledge of Greek authors and philosophy which qualified him for dealing with learned Gentiles and appealing to their own writers (Acts 17:18-28. Aratus; 1 Cor. 15:33, Menander; Titus 1:12, Epimenides). Here too he learned the Cilician trade of making tents of the goats' hair cloth called "cilicium" (Acts 18:3); not that his father was in straitened circumstances, but Jewish custom required each child, however wealthy the parents might be, to learn a trade. He possessed the Roman citizenship from birth (Acts 22:28), and hence, when he commenced ministering among Gentiles, he preferred to be known by his Roman name Paul rather than by his Hebrew name Saul. His main education (probably after passing his first 12 years at Tarsus (Acts 26:4-5) *"among his own nation." Alexandrinus, Vaticanus, Sinaiticus manuscripts read "and" before "at Jerusalem") was at Jerusalem "at the feet of Gamaliel (which see?)*, taught according to the perfect manner of the law of the fathers" (Acts 22:3). Thus the three elements of the world's culture met in him: Roman citizenship, Grecian culture, Hebrew religion.[9]

It is with this background we begin to get an idea of why God chose such a man to be the ambassador to the Gentiles at such a time.

THE "WHY" OR "PURPOSE"

As we have seen, Paul had the background to equip him for the task of propagating the fulfillment of Genesis 12:3c and Isaiah 52:15.

Paul saw the Abrahamic Covenant as the beginning of the Gospel proclaimed; writing: "And the Scripture, foreseeing that God would justify the Gentiles by faith, preached the gospel beforehand to Abraham, saying, All the nations shall be blessed in you." [10]

Paul believed, as expressed in Romans 15:21, that he was the fulfillment of Isaiah 52:15, as quoted here: "They who have no news of Him shall see, and they who have not heard shall understand." If we begin to connect the dots, we will see a history and time that is ready for the "time of the Gentiles" to be fulfilled (Romans 11:25). In addition, because the Gentiles have no background in the things of God, how should the Gospel or the things of God be presented for understanding? I believe that the book of Romans provides the answer, and I believe I am in good company: "John Drane proposes a theory on the purpose of Romans by analyzing the Roman Church sociologically. The purpose of Romans, however, is not found in Rome but in the life of Paul: He is making a conscious effort to convince himself as well as his opponents that it is possible to articulate a theology which is at once anti-legalistic without also being intrinsically antinomian (p. 234). His basis for seeing a fragmented Roman Church is not wholly convincing." [11] Are John Drane or I alone in this line of thinking? Consider the following comments:

> In searching for a statement of the purpose of Romans that is more reflective of the author's (and the text's) concerns and viewpoints, it would seem that Paul's status as a pioneer evangelist and church planter could hardly be overemphasized. In a real sense he was an "incidental theologian" when his missionary work demanded it. If this is accurate, it would certainly seem nearer the mark to start from a missiological, cross-cultural reference point rather than a theological, conscience-oriented perspective in viewing Paul's epistles. In other words as a whole they should be more outward looking than inward-looking and more activistic than introspective in basic orientation. While they speak of

individual salvation, they tend to emphasize the salvation of the peoples of the world. Rather than absolutizing one particular model of salvation, Paul, as a sensitive, cross-cultural missionary, probably viewed salvation from the perspective of several different models as he encountered different people-groups (e.g., power-over-spirits perspective, new creation perspective, forensic perspective, etc.). Rather than ending up with a "justification by faith" core for Paul's theology (and then reading all his epistles through this lens), a more global theme would seem to be appropriate. The redemptive-historical approach to Paul appears to be a healthy step in this direction.[12]

If you couple this fact with Paul addressing not a single local church but a group of Christians in Rome, it becomes more reasonable to see Paul's letter as a pastor teaching the Gentile group as a whole. The evidence of this can be seen in Romans Chapters 15 and 16. "But I have written very boldly to you on some points, so as to remind you again, because of the grace that was given me from God, to be a minister of Christ Jesus to the Gentiles, ministering as a priest the gospel of God, that my offering of the Gentiles might become acceptable, sanctified by the Holy Spirit." [13]

Paul is addressing Christians he has already come in contact with and was brought to Rome collectively through historical circumstances; this observation comes from Paul's greetings to multiple groups in the form of individuals and house churches in Romans Chapter 16. Jamieson, Fausset, and Brown make these comments on Romans 16:15:

> Salute Philologus, and Julia, Nereus, and his sister, and Olympas, and all the saints which are with them. These have been thought to be the names of ten less notable Christians

than those already named. But this will hardly be supposed if it be observed that they are divided into two pairs of five each, and that after the first of these pairs it is added, "and the brethren which are with them," while after the second pair we have the words, "and all the saints which are with them." This, perhaps, hardly means that each of the five in both pairs had 'a church at his house,' else probably this would have been more expressly said. But at least it would seem to indicate that they were each a center of some few Christians who met at his house—it may be for further instruction, for prayer, for missionary purposes, or for some other Christian objects. These little peeps into the rudimental forms which Christian fellowship first took in the great cities, though too indistinct for more than conjecture, are singularly interesting. Our apostle would seem to have been kept minutely informed as to the state of the Roman church, both as to its membership and its varied activities, probably by Priscilla and Aquila.[14]

Because Paul has known these people in the past and has provided them some teaching, it is my suggestion that Paul is continuing where he felt, he left off in his association with them. This leaves us a book or letter that offers wider instruction than one written to address the problems of a group, or to combat false teaching as he has done in other letters, but is providing wisdom and information for their edification and fellowship with Christ, and one with another, for there is now no difference between Jew and Greek (non-Jews) in Jesus Christ. Therefore, Paul is now, through this letter, bridging a social and religious gap by bringing instruction and explanation of their faith in Christ as it related to them from the Jewish beginning. D. B. Garlington states:

> Unique to the whole of pre-Christian Greek literature and to Paul himself, the phrase ὑπακοὴ πίστεως, occurring in

Rom. 1:5 and 16:26, gives voice to the design of the apostle's missionary gospel. Within Romans itself the phrase is invested with a twofold significance. For one, against the backdrop of faith's obedience in Jewish literature, these words assume a decidedly polemical thrust: the covenant fidelity of God's ancient people (Israel) is now a possibility apart from assuming the identity of that people. Dunn then is right that the phrase neatly summarizes Paul's apologetic in the Roman letter.[15]

It is with this in mind we will begin to look at the Theology of Romans, perhaps with a slightly different perspective.

AN OUTLINE OF ROMANS

We will follow the suggested outline of *Wiersbe's Expository Outline of the New Testament* for convenience and organization of thoughts in our discussion on this topic. The following is the outline purposed:

Suggested Outline of Romans [16]

Introduction (1:1-17)
    A. Salutation (1:1-7)
    B. Explanation (1:8-17)

I. Sin (1:18-3:20 - Righteousness Needed)
    A. The Gentiles under sin (1:18-32)
    B. The Jews under sin (2:1-3:8)
    C. The whole world under sin (3:9-20)

II. Salvation (3:21-5:21 - Righteousness Imputed)
    A. Justification explained (3:21-31)
    B. Justification expressed: the example of Abraham (4)

THE BOOK OF ROMANS: AN ESSAY PERSPECTIVE FOR THE CHURCH

    C. Justification experienced (5)

III. Sanctification (6-8 - Righteousness Imparted)
    A. Our new position in Christ (6)
    B. Our new problem in the flesh (7)
    C. Our new power in the Spirit (8)

IV. Sovereignty (9-11 - Righteousness Rejected)
    A. Israel's past election (9)
    B. Israel's present rejection (10)
    C. Israel's future redemption (11)

V. Service (12:1-15:13 - Righteousness Practiced)
    A. Consecration to God (12)
    B. Subjection to authority (13)
    C. Consideration for the weak (14:1-15:13)

VI. Conclusion (15:14-16:27)
    A. Paul's faithfulness in the ministry (15:14-21)
    B. Paul's future in the ministry (15:22-33) 121
    C. Paul's friends in the ministry (16:1-23)
    D. Final benediction (16:24-27)

From the introduction of this letter, we begin to see an explanation of purpose come together. D. B. Garlington puts this in perspective for us:

> Unique to the whole of pre-Christian Greek literature and to Paul himself, the phrase ὑπακοὴ πίστεως, occurring in Rom. 1:5 and 16:26, gives voice to the design of the apostle's missionary gospel. Within Romans itself the phrase is invested with a twofold significance. For one, against the

backdrop of faith's obedience in Jewish literature, these words assume a decidedly polemical thrust: the covenant fidelity of God's ancient people (Israel) is now a possibility apart from assuming the identity of that people. Dunn then is right that the phrase neatly summarizes Paul's apologetic in the Roman letter.

From another point of view, Rom. 1:5 can be looked upon as a programmatic statement of the main purpose of the Roman letter. For this reason Dunn again is correct in writing: 'To clarify what faith is and its importance to his gospel is one of Paul's chief objectives in this letter.' In order to appreciate the point, it will be necessary briefly to relate the importance of faith to another purpose of the letter, viz., 'to redraw the boundaries which marked out the people of God.' Whereas before to be a member of the covenant people was to live within the boundary set by the law, the eschatological people have assumed a new corporate identity. And since there is now "no distinction" between Jew and Gentile (1:16—17; 2:11; 10:12; etc.), Paul endeavors in Romans to expound the ethical and social expression of this new corporate entity.[17]

Within Paul's explanation of his letter, he recognizes the importance of their testimony throughout the world; and wishes to help them to be more settled in their faith. (Romans 1:11) From this explanation, he begins to teach the concepts we noted in our outline.

Righteousness Needed

The Gentiles need to understand righteousness within God's concept of sin; and ignorance is no excuse (Romans 1:20). Paul then turns to the Jews in Chapter 2: You (Jews) to are without excuse, because you know better, having knowledge but do not practice what you know to be true. (Romans 2:1-5) In Chapter 3, Paul concludes that both Jew and Greek (Gentile) are equally under condemnation; that no one is righteous (Romans 3:10). Imputed righteousness is therefore required to attain justification with God.

RIGHTEOUSNESS IMPUTED

Within the context of Jewish Law, we have fallen short, but by grace, through the redemptive work of Christ, we can now be justified in the sight of God (Romans 3:21-25).

Because the Scriptures were first given to the Jews, the new doctrine Paul is conveying must be explained in the context of the Old Testament patriarchs in which it all started. Thus, we have Chapter 4, the foundation for the concepts of redemption and justification, starting with the Abrahamic Covenant and Abraham's demonstration of faith.

Then in Chapter 5, we have justification experienced, an explanation of its benefits to us as believers (Romans 5: 9-11). In the remaining part of this chapter, we have Paul explaining once again the connection between the law, sin, transgression, and justification. This then leads us to the concept of righteousness imparted.

RIGHTEOUSNESS IMPARTED

The result of righteousness imputed is our newfound position in Christ. Because this is a new concept, Paul now takes three chapters to expound its reality and importance, concluding in Chapter 8 by introducing a second new concept: the power available through the indwelling Holy Spirit. He refers to these concepts in Chapter 16 as the revelation of the mysteries hidden from ages past. His letters to the Ephesians and the Colossians further clarify these concepts.

> ... that by revelation there was made known to me the mystery, as I wrote before in brief. And by referring to this,

when you read you can understand my insight into the mystery of Christ, which in other generations was not made known to the sons of men, as it has now been revealed to His holy apostles and prophets in the Spirit; to be specific, that the Gentiles are fellow heirs and fellow members of the body, and fellow partakers of the promise in Christ Jesus through the gospel, of which I was made a minister, according to the gift of God's grace which was given to me according to the working of His power.[18]

Of this church I was made a minister according to the stewardship from God bestowed on me for your benefit, that I might fully carry out the preaching of the word of God, that is, the mystery which has been hidden from the past ages and generations; but has now been manifested to His saints, to whom God willed to make known what is the riches of the glory of this mystery among the Gentiles, which is Christ in you, the hope of glory.[19]

These concepts are clearly based in Jeremiah 31:31-34:

Behold, days are coming, declares the Lord, when I will make a new covenant with the house of Israel and with the house of Judah, not like the covenant which I made with their fathers in the day I took them by the hand to bring them out of the land of Egypt, My covenant which they broke, although I was a husband to them, declares the Lord. But this is the covenant which I will make with the house of Israel after those days, declares the Lord, I will put My law within them, and on their heart I will write it; and I will be their God, and they shall be My people. And they shall not teach again, each man his neighbor and each man his brother, saying, 'Know the Lord,' for they shall all know Me, from the least of them to the greatest of them, declares the Lord, for I will forgive their iniquity, and their sin I will remember no more.

Here is where God describes his promise—a new covenant with Israel—into which the Christian church has been grafted, as described in Romans 11. Herbert Kann writes,

> The mystery of Israel's blindness is stated in Paul's letter to the Romans, Chapter 11, verses 25 to 27: "For I would not, brethren, that ye should be ignorant of this mystery, lest ye should be wise in your own conceits; that blindness in part is happened to Israel, until the fullness of the Gentiles be come in. And so all Israel shall be saved: as it is written, There shall come out of Zion the Deliverer, and shall turn away ungodliness from Jacob: for this is my covenant unto them, when I shall take away their sins." [20]

"Righteousness imparted," reveals the mystery of "Christ in you"—made possible as the Holy Spirit lives in us—bringing God's righteousness to our lives and making us worthy to be called his adopted sons. This process enables Gentiles to become part of the body of Christ—the living universal Church. Arnold Fruchtenbaum speaks of the mysteries in these terms:

> The third evidence is the mystery character of the Church. A mystery is a New Testament truth not revealed in the Old Testament (Ephesians 3:3—5, 9; Colossians 1:26—27). While Scripture does not call the Church itself a mystery, it so labels a number of features that are unique to the Church. There are four such features: (a) The body concept of Jewish and Gentile believers united into one body is a mystery (Ephesians 3:1—12). (b) The doctrine of Christ indwelling every believer, the Christ in you concept, is a mystery

(Colossians 1:24—27; 2:10—19; 3:4, 11). (c) The concept of the Church as the Bride of Christ is a mystery (Ephesians 5:22—32). (d) The Rapture with its corollary events of the resurrection of the dead and the translation of the living is called a mystery in 1 Corinthians 15:50—58. These four mysteries, each relevant only to the Church, show that the Church itself is a mystery and distinct from Israel.[21]

Righteousness Rejected

Paul takes these mysteries and ties them into righteousness rejected. The Jews were clueless as to these "mysteries revealed," so Paul's mission was to explain these mysteries to the Gentiles; giving them an opportunity to participate in the fulfillment of God's covenants. Charles Lincoln expresses it this way:

> Israel, as a nation, rejected Christ when He came. His blood was that of the New Covenant, as the Seed of Promise; but, as Israel rejected Him, their enjoyment of the benefits of the saving work of the promised Seed awaits their repentance and faith in Him and their realization of the New Covenant in His blood, which according to Hebrews 8:7—13, is still future in Israel's experience. In the meantime, the New Covenant is ministered unto the church (2 Corinthians 3:6), and the universal blessings of the Abrahamic Covenant are being realized particularly by the Gentiles; but universal blessing to the Gentiles will be even more completely realized when Israel comes into the full blessing of the New Covenant, which is provided for in the blood of Christ and will be established with the nation "in that day" (Acts 15:14ff). In the present day He is "visiting the Gentiles to take out of them a people for His name" (v. 14); afterward He turns to Israel and re-establishes that people as a nation, through the building

again of the tabernacle of David (v. 16); there will be widespread blessing on "all the Gentiles, upon whom his name is called" (v. 17). The Church did not exist in Old Testament times. Israel was not the Old Testament Church as some erroneously claim without Scriptural foundation." ... The church is a mystery hid in God in times past; it is composed principally of "a people taken out of the Gentiles for Christ's name." It is formed during the interim of Israel's rejection of her Messiah, Christ, the promised seed. This Covenant of Abraham is, therefore, predominantly related to Israel, though it contains the universal Gospel-promise of Christ the Redeemer.[22]

The question could be raised. Why Chapters 9 through 11? Paul may reveal the answer to us as he writes,

I say then, they did not stumble so as to fall, did they? May it never be! But by their transgression salvation has come to the Gentiles, to make them jealous. Now if their transgression be riches for the world and their failure be riches for the Gentiles, how much more will their fulfillment be! But I am speaking to you who are Gentiles. Inasmuch then as I am an apostle of Gentiles, I magnify my ministry, if somehow I might move to jealousy my fellow countrymen and save some of them. For if their rejection be the reconciliation of the world, what will their acceptance be but life from the dead? And if the first piece of dough be holy, the lump is also; and if the root be holy, the branches are too. But if some of the branches were broken off, and you, being a wild olive, were grafted in among them and became partaker with them of the rich root of the olive tree, do not be arrogant toward the branches; but if you are arrogant, remember that it is not you who supports the root, but the root supports you.

You will say then, "Branches were broken off so that I might be grafted in." Quite right, they were broken off for their unbelief, but you stand by your faith. Do not be conceited, but fear; for if God did not spare the natural branches, neither will He spare you. Behold then the kindness and severity of God; to those who fell, severity, but to you, God's kindness, if you continue in His kindness; otherwise you also will be cut off. And they also, if they do not continue in their unbelief, will be grafted in; for God is able to graft them in again. For if you were cut off from what is by nature a wild olive tree, and were grafted contrary to nature into a cultivated olive tree, how much more shall these who are the natural branches be grafted into their own olive tree? [23]

Within this passage, there are two important concepts. One is Paul's explanation for the rejection of "righteousness imparted" and how the Gentiles were tied to that rejection and became the beneficiaries of being grafted in. The second is Paul's admonishing about possible pride spats between the two groups: with the Jews taking a sense of pride in their heritage with Abraham (John 8:31-39); and the Gentiles perhaps feeling a little proud of being chosen over Israel in the promise that was given (Romans 9:24-30).

It was through these circumstances the Gentiles were given an explanation as to why, from a historical perspective, they have a position in Christ, and told not to be arrogant in their newfound position, giving perhaps a reason for conflict between the two groups. "Paul warned the Gentiles that they were obligated to Israel, and therefore they dared not boast of their new spiritual position (Romans 11:18-21). The Gentiles entered God's plan because of faith, and not because of any good they had done. Paul was discussing the Gentiles collectively, and not the individual experience of one believer or another." [24]

RIGHTEOUSNESS PRACTISED

Paul transitions into Chapter 12 through 15:13: righteousness practiced, which makes perfect sense because of his understanding of the Gospel and God's grace. He rightfully understood that, as new creatures in Christ, we are expected to walk in the shadow of God and represent Him through good works, and thus the reason for instructions in "righteousness practiced." His message to the Ephesians summarizes this thought: "For by grace you have been saved through faith; and that not of yourselves, it is the gift of God; not as a result of works, that no one should boast. For we are His workmanship, created in Christ Jesus for good works, which God prepared beforehand, that we should walk in them." [25]

Paul hits on the topics relevant to not only his day but ours as well. Topics such as, our sanctification or separation from the world system, which produces holy living, fulfilling God's commandment to be "Holy as I am Holy" (Lev. 19:2); honor God's established principles of authority (John 10:18; 17:2; 19:10-11); and think of others in life and not just yourself, another principle already established by God (Romans 13:9-10). All solid teachings for everyday life, which Christ said he came that we might have it more abundantly through righteous living (John 10:10).

CONCLUSION

It is evident from our discussion that God created such a man and time to spread the Gospel of Jesus Christ, by proclaiming the mysteries hidden in times past, and by God's will, has now made known the new concept of "Christ in you", and as the Scriptures add, "the hope of glory" (Colossians 1:25-27).

Paul's background, his birth, family, education, and life experience equipped him to minister and spread the word of God among the Gentiles so that the Gentiles would in turn carry that message around the known world. Yes, God had a plan; and the book of Romans reveals that plan and its instructions in how to live in the world, apart from the Jewish law, through God's righteousness in Christ Jesus. The International Standard Bible Encyclopedia includes these supporting comments:

> It has been held by some great students, notably Lightfoot and Hort, that the main purpose of Romans was to reconcile the opposing "schools" in the church, and that its exposition of the salvation of the individual is secondary only. The present writer cannot take this view. Read the Epistle from its spiritual center, so to speak, and is not the perspective very different? The apostle is always conscious of the collective aspect of the Christian life, an aspect vital to its full health. But is he not giving his deepest thought, animated by his own experience of conviction and conversion, to the sinful man's relation to eternal law, to redeeming grace, and to a coming glory? It is the question of personal salvation which with Paul seems to us to live and move always in the depth of his argument, even when Christian polity and policy is the immediate theme.[26]

It is my view that Romans should not be seen as focused on solving divisions in the church, but as an extension of Paul's life; as one whom God prepared and ordained for informing, guiding and instructing the Gentiles, for a better understanding of the gospel and their everyday life in Christ. Let me close with a final summary thought from the Apostle Paul:

> Therefore remember, that formerly you, the Gentiles in the flesh, who are called 'Uncircumcision' by the so-called 'Circumcision,' which is performed in the flesh by human hands—remember that you were at that time separate from

Christ, excluded from the commonwealth of Israel, and strangers to the covenants of promise, having no hope and without God in the world. But now in Christ Jesus you who formerly were far off have been brought near by the blood of Christ. For He Himself is our peace, who made both groups into one, and broke down the barrier of the dividing wall, by abolishing in His flesh the enmity, which is the Law of commandments contained in ordinances, that in Himself He might make the two into one new man, thus establishing peace, and might reconcile them both in one body to God through the cross, by it having put to death the enmity.[27]

Chapter Endnotes

1. Robert L. Cate, *A History of the New Testament and its Times* (Nashville: Broadman Press, 1991), 52.

2. Sean Freyne, *The World of the New Testament* (Wilmington: Michael Glazier, Inc., 1980), 5

3. Eduard Lohse, *The New Testament Environment*, By John E. Steely (Nashville: Abingdon, 1976), 232.

4. Cate, *A History of the New Testament and its Times*, 75.

5. Lohse, *The New Testament Environment*, 77-82.

6. Marcel Simon, *Jewish Sects at the Time of Jesus* (Philadelphia: Fortress Press, 1967), 33-36.

7. *Fausset's Bible Dictionary*, s. v. "Pharisees", Electronic Database, [CD Rom] (Seattle: Biblesoft, ©1998, 2003, 2006.)

8. *Encyclopedia Britannica 2003 Deluxe Edition*, s. v. "Claudius", Electronic Database, [CD-ROM/DVD] ©1994-2002.

9. Fausset's Bible Dictionary, s. v. "Paul", Electronic Database, [CD-ROM] (Seattle: Biblesoft, ©1998, 2003, 2006.)

10. Gal. 3:8 NASB (New American Standard Bible)

11. Scott McKnight, "Pauline Studies: Essays Presented to Professor F. F. Bruce on His 70th Birthday," *Journal of the Evangelical Theological Society* Vol. 24:3 (September 1981; 2002): 286. available from The Theological Journal Library, vol. 1-5, [CD-ROM] (Garland: Galaxie Software, ©2000-2006).

THE BOOK OF ROMANS: AN ESSAY PERSPECTIVE FOR THE CHURCH

12. Walter B. Russell III, "An Alternative Suggestion for the Purpose of Romans," Bibliotheca Sacra Vol. 145 (April 1988; 2002):179-180. Available from *The Theological Journal Library*, vol. 1-5, [CD-ROM] (Garland: Galaxie Software, ©2000-2006).

13. Rom. 15:15-16 NASB (New American Standard Bible)

14. *Jamieson, Fausset, and Brown Commentary*, "Romans 16:15: Salute Philologus, and Julia, Nereus, and his sister, and Olympas, and all the saints which are with them", Electronic Database, [CD-ROM] (Seattle: Biblesoft, © 1997, 2003, 2005, 2006.

15. D. B. Garlington, "The Obedience of Faith in the Letter to the Romans. Part I: The Meaning of ὑπακοὴ πίστεως (Rom 1:5; 16:26)," *Westminster Theological Journal* Vol. 52:2 (Fall 1990): 201. Available from The Theological Journal Library, vol. 1-5, [CD-ROM] (Garland: Galaxie Software, ©2000-2006).

16. *Wiersbe's Expository Outlines on the New Testament*, "Romans", © 1992 by Chariot Victor Publishing, an imprint of Cook Communication Ministries, Electronic Database, [CD-ROM] (Seattle: Biblesoft, ©1998, 2003, 2006.)

17. D. B. Garlington, "The Obedience of Faith in the Letter to the Romans. Part I: The Meaning of ὑπακοὴ πίστεως (Rom 1:5; 16:26)," *Westminster Theological Journal* Vol. 52:2 (Fall 1990): 201-202.

18. Eph. 3:3-8 NASB (New American Standard Bible)

19. Col. 1:25-27 NASB (New American Standard Bible)

20. Herbert Kann, "The History of Israel's Blindness: The Mystery of It," *Bibliotheca Sacra* Vol. 94:376 (October 1937): 442. Available from The Theological Journal Library, vol. 1-5, [CD-ROM] (Garland: Galaxie Software, ©2000-2006).

21. Arnold Fruchtenbaum, "Israelology: Part 3 of 6" *Chafer Theological Seminary Journal* Vol. 5:4 (September 1999; 2002): 39. available from The Theological Journal Library, vol. 1-5, [CD-ROM] (Garland: Galaxie Software, ©2000-2006).

22. Charles Fred Lincoln, "The Biblical Covenants," *Bibliotheca Sacra* Vol. 100:398 (April 1943; 2002): 322-323. available from The Theological Journal Library, vol. 1-5, [CD-ROM] (Garland: Galaxie Software, ©2000-2006).

23. Rom. 11:11-24 NASB (New American Standard Bible)

24. *The Bible Exposition Commentary*, s. v. "The olive tree (vv. 16b-24)," © 1989 by Chariot Victor

25. Eph. 2:8-10 NASB (New American Standard Bible)

26. *International Standard Bible Encyclopedia*, s. v. "Romans, Epistle to the," Electronic Database, [CD-ROM] (Seattle: Biblesoft, ©1998, 2003, 2006.)

27. Eph. 2:11-16 NASB (New American Standard Bible)

STUDY GUIDE SUGGESTIONS

I have written this book as a tool for Christian discipleship, to help Christians understand foundational truths about their faith, and, providing some knowledge to the body of Christ, for the purpose of bringing an element of stability through sound reasoning based on God's Word.

Either way, you may find that group discussions offer a helpful setting for working through it; so I have included some suggestions to facilitate these discussions.

The key to a good discussion is to start with the Preface and Introduction pages, which will provide you with some context for what you are reading. The key to my books is the Scriptures, which are the source for understanding God's truth, and I hope you find the following suggestions to be helpful.

1. When starting this study, plan to pre-assign a reading schedule for the group to follow, so they can read the material before they come to each meeting.

2. Research the endnotes at the end of each chapter. The websites listed may offer additional information on the topics noted.

3. Read a segment or sub-section aloud; pause for comments or questions.

4. Another option is to look up all the Scriptures as referenced and see how they fit into the context of the subject being discussed. Then ask if these Scriptures are relevant, or how they clarify anyone's understanding of the topic or the concepts.

5. Other helpful questions may be, Is this information new to anyone? Is this important or relevant to my life? Does this information offer a wider context for other important aspects of my life? Does this apply to other Scriptural concepts?

6. A good way to wrap up a discussion on any segment is to ask others to summarize what has been said in the book's content and within the discussion.

You may find these suggestions to help you to discover other approaches to discussion groups. But your preferred choices are ultimately between you and the Holy Spirit, who is our ultimate teacher.

To quote the Apostle Paul: "The grace of the Lord Jesus Christ, and the love of God, and the fellowship of the Holy Spirit, be with you all." (2 Corinthians 13:14)

ACKNOWLEDGMENTS

I want to thank the Lord for bringing this project to my mind and for helping me to put this material in perspective for others to see and to use for their own edification.

I also want to thank and express my appreciation to my Australian friend Noel Mitaxa, for his participation in the First's editing of the original work this book is revising, along with providing helpful suggestions to that work, towards a clearer presentation of the original work to the reading public worldwide.

ABOUT THE AUTHOR

Reid Ashbaucher born in the United States, holds a B.A. degree in Comprehensive Bible, an M.A. degree in Christian Theology, and has completed some postgraduate work towards a Ph.D. in Religious Studies.

Reid has been a believer in Jesus Christ for over 55 years. While experiencing life through secular fields of Military Service, Business Ownership, and Radio Broadcast Engineering, Reid has served in local Christian churches as deacon, teacher, and pulpit supply.

Throughout his life, Reid has sought to promote the Word of God as the source of true reality in all things. This reality can be summed up in Jesus Christ's words as He states: "Therefore everyone who hears these words of Mine, and acts upon them, may be compared to a wise man, who built his house upon the rock" (Matthew 7:24; NASB).

ADDITIONAL WORKS BY THE AUTHOR

- *Made in the Image of God: Understanding the Nature of God and Mankind in a Changing World* (Third Revised Edition; 2020)

- *Dispensational Theology: A Textbook for Eschatology in the Twenty-First Century* (June 2019)

www.ingramcontent.com/pod-product-compliance
Lightning Source LLC
Chambersburg PA
CBHW031115080526
44587CB00011B/985